A Little Closer to Home

How I Found the Calm After the Storm

Ginger Zee

**HYPERION
AVENUE**

LOS ANGELES • NEW YORK

To Ben, my love.
While the healing and hard work have been
on me, you gave me the love, support, and a home
I now know I deserve. Thank you, forever.

This book contains discussion of mental illness and suicide.

If you or someone you know is in crisis, there is help available. Call the
National Suicide Prevention Lifeline at **1-800-273-TALK (8255)**, or text
the Crisis Text Line (**text HOME to 741741**). Both services are free and
available twenty-four hours a day, seven days a week.

First Edition, October 2021
10 9 8 7 6 5 4 3 2 1
FAC-021131-21239
Printed in the United States of America

Library of Congress Cataloging-in-Publication: 2021935659

ISBN 978-1-368-04200-0

Reinforced binding
Visit ginger-zee.com

Contents

Introduction 1

CHAPTER ONE The Drain 17

CHAPTER TWO It Really Doesn't Matter and Nobody Cares 27

CHAPTER THREE Divorce 43

CHAPTER FOUR Pam 55

CHAPTER FIVE Labels 75

CHAPTER SIX Anorexia 91

CHAPTER SEVEN Camp Hug-a-Lot 107

CHAPTER EIGHT Sex 119

CHAPTER NINE Sexy Mama 133

CHAPTER TEN "Likely" Rape 147

CHAPTER ELEVEN My First Meditation 161

CHAPTER TWELVE The Choice 169

CHAPTER THIRTEEN Oh Yeah 191

CHAPTER FOURTEEN Cat-5 Risk Assessment 211

CHAPTER FIFTEEN The Mask 237

CHAPTER SIXTEEN John...Again 249

CHAPTER SEVENTEEN A Long Road Ahead 259

CHAPTER EIGHTEEN The Clouds Don't Last Forever 269

INTRODUCTION

This is a book about healing. A deep healing in a woman, who ten years ago found herself in a mental health hospital, but is now thriving and finding her identity.

She is me and this introduction changed just months before final print because after I reread the manuscript and shared it with other people, I realized the book isn't really about the healing itself, but about the process of healing, and most importantly the hard work that is required before and after healing.

After my therapist read this book, he said something so poignant to me that I had to include it. Even he, who had been with me through this whole journey after my mental health hospitalization, had not realized how much I had been through and more importantly how much I have overcome. Reading it all in one sitting in such a condensed fashion changed the story for him and for me.

Instead of being concerned about releasing more deep,

dark secrets for the world to know and to judge me on, I know that these "secrets" are my secret weapons.

Sharing these secrets is power and gives me an instant jolt of connection to other people who are on their own mental health odyssey. My transparency in my first book helped other people but also gave me sovereignty over my own narrative. It's true that I will never be 100 percent cured of all of my issues, but I have proven that dedication to healing is effective. I am living proof! Goodness, I sound like an infomercial. But just like the Flowbee had an infomercial, this is a process that works and will hopefully last you a lifetime. (My dad still has the Flowbee he bought in the 1980s to cut our hair and it still works. It is also back in style to have a Flowbee. I can't believe it.)

Every time I charge myself with writing a chapter, committing more time to finding other ways to meditate, or even forcing myself to sit on my couch and launch the Zoom therapy session that I "don't really need at the moment," it uncovers something else I do need to work on. But that something else, I can now put in a HEALING, solution-based narrative. One of the most important topics I will cover in this book is how to address trauma. For now, I will equate mental and emotional trauma to a wound.

Prior to doing this hard work, my way of dealing with a wound would be to immediately cover it with dirt and pretend it never happened. You can imagine how that turned out. While I have been navigating the deep infections and twisted scars that evolved from the uncared-for wounds of my life, I now spend much of my time gathering the tools that will help me make the inevitable next wound a cleaner and quicker heal.

Societally, we put a pretty hefty emphasis on our physical health, focusing so much time, money, and thought into how we can make ourselves *look* good. I've taken that energy, once reserved solely for physical health, and shifted it to mental health, where I put time, energy, and money into making my *brain* look good (feel good). Every week, every day, I do something to make it cleaner, stronger, and better, and it is working. I hope that with this book, using my secret weapons as the fuel, we can keep encouraging each other to put in the effort and find the solutions that work for us. We all deserve it.

You go to the gym for two weeks, start seeing the benefits, and then quit and expect it all to stick. *Mental* health is the same as physical health. It requires effort, but the payoff is so worth it.

My name is Ginger. I am the chief meteorologist at ABC News, the first woman to hold that title at a major network. I have covered nearly every recent giant weather event from Hurricane Katrina to the latest Category-5 hurricane (Michael), and Category-4 hurricane (Laura). I've had the honor of taking people around the world on amazing adventures like paragliding off the Himalayas with vultures eating out of my hand, to most recently telling a climate-change story in Africa at Victoria Falls. I was on *Dancing with the Stars*, I have a spectacular husband, two young boys, and I have attempted suicide. Twice.

That last part is not the most common component to an introduction and certainly doesn't make it into my bio at work, but it has become an important part of my personal prologue for the past few years. Three years ago, I finally found real healing in a place I did not expect. I wrote a book, not just about my first suicide attempt, but about my decades'-long battle with depression and the tools I have learned in order to live with it. I didn't have a clue how much more mental mending it would bring me, but now that it has, I want to share more. And I want to share it with you.

I'm still a little surprised I became a memoir writer. *Memoir.* What a strange word. There was no part of me that wanted to write one, that's for sure. My entire life I had told myself I wasn't a writer. However, when I was pregnant with my first son, we looked high and low for a good baby book about weather and just couldn't find one. I figured I could handle writing a baby book, twenty pages of large font and mostly pictures, especially with my platform as a chief meteorologist. I fortuitously met with a wonderful woman named Wendy Lefkon and her team at Disney Publishing. When I told them about the character and stories I wanted to tell, they told me that they fit a preteen, chapter-book audience better. As we discussed how the trilogy of Helicity would play out, I began sharing my personal stories, since many of Helicity's adventures would be based on my own life. When talking about my experience covering Hurricane Katrina, I said, well, that was when I was engaged and became a runaway bride. Oh, and that blizzard was when a homeless lady chased me under a bridge in Chicago.

Through the self-deprecating style I usually tell stories with, Wendy and her team convinced me that the book I really needed to write was a memoir about my life, the storms and adventure. As soon as I started writing, it was impossible to ignore my mental-health challenges.

So yes, I went in to write a baby book about rainbows and sunshine and came out first with a book for adults about suicide and depression.

I was really surprised at how much I enjoyed the entire process of writing the book. But the night before *Natural Disaster* went to print, I started thinking about the opening line, in which I write about checking myself into the psychiatric ward at Columbia University Medical Center. My husband and I were lying in bed and I couldn't sleep. I turned on the light and nudged him awake.

"Bean, I think I should call this off. I think I said too much in the book. What if I lose my job?"

He saw that I was panicking, but he didn't miss a beat. He

reminded me that it was good to be nervous because it meant the book wasn't just going to be some nice story about a nice girl. This book was going to be about the true me—messy, deeply faulted, and fallible. I thought back to the moment I had told Wendy's team that I really didn't want this book to have the typical cover: a photo of me, smiling in a pastel sweater. Because that was *not* what my book was about. That would not be a book worth sharing. This was.

After remembering that and listening to my sage husband, suddenly I could breathe again. For the first time in my life, I was letting go. Letting go of caring what other people think and letting go of working so hard to be the person I thought everybody wanted me to be.

After my book was published, people started divulging their stories to me, sharing their deepest secrets and their own personal storms. These people also had more questions. I began to write this follow-up book aimed to help answer those questions, but as I started writing I figured out that I was far from "cured." I decided to go back to therapy full time so I could learn more to share with all of you. I also realized there was a major part of my life I did not share in the first book that was integral to my story.

That's why this book is called *A Little Closer to Home*. When I got the job at *Good Morning America*, I knew I was going to need a cue phrase to toss to the local affiliates. I had grown up watching Al Roker say *in your neck of the woods* and I put a lot of thought into finding just the right slogan that I would want to say forever, because I intended on having the job for a very long time. I came up with *a little closer to home.*

When I was struggling for a title for this book, my husband suggested my catchphrase, and it is the only title that works. But this book isn't just a little closer to home. It is a *lot* closer to home.

The real impetus for going back to therapy came at a surprising time. I had started my morning like any other, met with the weather team, discussed our headlines and what images we would share to tell the big weather story, got through hair and makeup, did promos for our affiliates, and settled in at my makeshift desk on the studio floor. It's actually more of a piece of glossy whiteboard that is almost flush with the back of a large wall on the set in the wings of GMA. It is right where all correspondents, producers, and guests enter the studio. With my back to that door I didn't need to see, I could feel that this was a busy news day with the number of people that were crowding near the entrance.

Christine Blasey-Ford had given her testimony at the Kavanaugh hearings. The top of our show, the part we call the *cold open,* featured part of her chilling statement on the stand. The first story was full of her words:

"I am here today not because I want to be, I am

terrified. . . . I understand and appreciate the importance of you hearing from me directly about what happened to me and the impact that it has had on my life and on my family. . . .

"I don't have all the answers and I don't remember as much as I would like to. I drank one beer. Brett and Mark were drunk. I was pushed onto the bed and Brett got on top of me. Brett groped me and tried to take off my clothes. They were drunkenly laughing during the attack. I was too afraid and ashamed to tell anyone these details. I convinced myself that because Brett did not rape me, I should just move on and pretend that it didn't happen. I did the best to ignore the memory of the assault."

I heard Christine Blasey-Ford's voice echo in my ear and then worm deep into my brain and memory. Her intimate description of sexual assault was so vivid and hit more than a little close to home. My cheeks flushed, I looked around to see how many people were in the studio because I knew I was going to cry. The tears started flowing and I couldn't stop them. I didn't want to. I knew in that moment it was important to feel. No matter what happened at the hearing, I felt that testimony evoke emotion and trauma in me that I had not addressed but knew I needed to. I realized that not only had I never dealt with my experience of rape, but it had spiraled into years of other traumatic events and a horrible habit of ignoring them all.

I didn't mention my second suicide attempt in the last book because I wasn't ready to talk about what happened right before I tried to take my own life.

I had an abortion.

There, I said it. It's definitely not included in that work bio. It's not something any of us talk about, but I kind of feel like we need to. Especially because it's what precipitated my second suicide attempt, and it was a powerful part of the mental-health spiral I rode to the bottom during the following ten years.

I am one of millions of women who have had and will have abortions. Nobody talks about it because it's not an easy discussion, and no one is allowed to talk about it before it automatically gets political. I don't want this book to be political. I want this book to be about a young woman who was forced to make a choice that would impact her life forever. I want this book to be about my abortion's physical and emotional toll on my life. This is neither a story shared to shame others nor is it in an effort to promote choice. No one talks about what can happen to you after "the choice"—for me it was a postpartum hormonal nosedive, the heaviest shame I have ever felt, and the lifelong guilt, acceptance, and forgiveness that I have needed to curate in order to survive. Not everyone has the same experience. But for those who might, I want them to have the education and support for options I didn't even know I had. I want everyone to know there is a simple step you can take to protect yourself from it ever happening to you. I am ready to be that person who finally talks about it and makes it okay to share so other young women don't have to be forced to make that choice.

While the number of abortions each year in America goes up and down and reporting is not mandatory, according to the Centers for Disease Control, it is estimated that in 2018 (the last year numbers were available at the time of this writing) more than six hundred thousand abortions were performed. Shouldn't the numbers alone give us permission and even a responsibility to talk about it?

It's been more than forty years since abortion was legalized, and as of this writing, it's still a lightning-rod issue in America. Many states and local municipalities have enacted anti-abortion laws in recent years. I want to repeat—this is not a book about politics or morality. In fact, I have made it a point to listen to both sides and I see the value in each side's stances and opinions. But neither side sounds like they have had an abortion because neither talks about what happens before and after to the woman in that position. Everyone is focused on the baby, the group of cells, or whatever side you are on would like to call it. But absolutely no one focuses on the woman carrying that embryo.

My hope with this book is to begin a substantive conversation on protection and education. There are several highly effective safe options for birth control including long-acting contraception, and it is important that women feel empowered to have these conversations with their health care provider. I truly believe that if I had access to a nearly fail-proof birth control method like the IUD before I got pregnant, I wouldn't have needed to have an abortion. If a young girl is raped by her uncle, an IUD won't save her from the mental torture and PTSD, but it could protect her from having a child born of that horrific start. Unfortunately, the knee-jerk reaction to providing protection for young people is still the argument that it's just going to lead to more promiscuity. In fact, statistics on sex education in high schools bear out the opposite conclusion.

According to Dr. Jennifer Ashton, a board-certified ob-gyn, nutritionist, and ABC News chief medical correspondent, "IUDs are underutilized in the United States. In many ways, they suffer from a public relations problem: in the 1980s and 1990s, IUDs were only recommended to women who had already had babies and who were in monogamous relationships—both pejorative and socially judgmental constructs imposed on women from the medical specialty of gynecology. This came about because the strings attached to the IUD were, at that time, made of a substance that potentially increased a woman's risk of pelvic infection if she contracted sexually transmitted infection. Today, it is now thankfully a very different situation for the IUD, though the damage from those times still persists. Today, the strings are made of a different material that does not act like a wick for bacteria. Also, the IUD is supported as an option by American College of Obstetricians and Gynecologists even in teenagers. It's not right for every teenager or woman, but it should be given as an option."

Women need more counseling and education about abortion as well. While I will not take a side on the morality of abortion, I'm concerned that if it's criminalized, women will go into hiding even more and there will be nobody there to help them. Something as simple as knowing about the postpartum drop in hormones after an abortion probably would have prevented me from trying to take my own life. I had nobody to talk to about the guilt and shame I would suffer from having an abortion that would affect every area of my life for the next two decades. All that time I thought I had to keep it a secret. My abortion was a giant lumbering elephant banging around in my psyche. Who knows how much less self-destructive pain I would have gone through if I'd dealt with it earlier? Who knows what I would have done if societally I wasn't told it is impossible to be a mother and advance in your career? I believe a big part of my damaging choices throughout most of my twenties was directly related to the guilt I felt after the abortion. Not my chaotic family life, parents' divorce, rape, etc. But the abortion.

We need to take this conversation out of the closet and give all women a chance to find the healing that I found in writing this book. Healing, forgiveness, and grace no matter what trauma someone has endured. I'll never be fully over it, but I have finally addressed it. In writing this book, I actually had to stop and focus on the therapy surrounding this choice I made seventeen years ago. Now I have given it the attention it deserves.

My first book was full of embarrassing, hopefully funny stories, and believe it or not, I still have more of those for the pages ahead. I'll also be bringing back my therapist, Dr. Wilson, because he has been my greatest teacher on my road to recovery. It's hard to find the perfect therapist, and if you haven't yet, please don't give up. It's worth the search to find the right combination of chemistry and faith that I have with Dr. Wilson. I worked with at least ten therapists before I met him after I was at an inpatient hospital at Columbia University Medical Center in New York City. Even a good therapist can't do the healing work for you, but they can be a trusted guide who knows the way and can help you find peace.

And for me, hospitalization and focusing on what type of therapy I needed was necessary. That's something I hope this book can do, too. I think we are all getting better about reducing the stigma around mental-health issues, but now the focus must be on the action taken after it is talked about and eliminating *that* stigma. We need to make hospitalization less frightening and more approachable. When you have a problem with your back, you go to your primary doctor, who then refers you to a specialist. We need this type of structure and attention to our mental health.

I wish I could tell you that I'm cured of either or both of the mental issues I've struggled with (anorexia and depression). I still have both, but I am highly functional and managing in the healthiest place I've ever been. I have a wonderful life and I am at peace, which was never something I even considered as a possibility. I want you to know you also deserve a great life, and you absolutely, without a doubt, deserve to be at peace. I purposefully did not use the word *happy* here, and you'll read why later.

Maybe you're reading this book because somebody recommended it. Maybe you heard about it somewhere and thought it was worth checking out. Maybe you just picked it up in a bookstore and two pages into it you're thinking, *Why the heck am I reading this?* I'll take any of those reasons, and I hope you'll stay with me until the end.

My story will not be exactly like anybody else's story. We all have different lives and different experiences that have shaped us into who we are. But I'm confident that we do share some things in common. Chances are, somehow you have been affected by mental illness. Maybe you've been diagnosed with anxiety, depression, or suicidal ideation. Maybe you just have funky days and can't pinpoint what's wrong. Maybe you have a friend or a family member who is suffering and you want to help. My first book taught me that; it was called *Natural Disaster, I Cover Them, I Am One*—because I am. But I am so not alone. Thousands of you have written to me to say how much you felt like you were reading your own story. I hope that happens again with this book and that we can all keep learning and healing together.

It's sad that my mental illness affected our entire family worse than it probably had to, but that's how mental illness works. The person suffering isn't the only one sucked into the darkness of the storm. Everybody who loves them gets caught up in it, too. To this day, I can't think about my suicide attempts without thinking about the fear in my parents' eyes when they rushed into my triage room at the hospital. Years later, they shared with me how after the suicide attempts, they were in constant fear of answering the phone because maybe somebody on the other end of the line would tell them that this time I'd succeeded. Now that I'm a mother, I can imagine how truly awful that must have been. But I no longer feel guilty for that because I finally realize that I was sick. I didn't choose to try to kill myself. As Vonnie Woodrick, from the group i understand and a leader in facilitating and understanding suicide, says, "Suicide is a side effect of depression, pain, or other mental illness."

And that's true; I was sick. I just found a way to manage

my illness. As Robin Roberts says, "Everybody's got something." We certainly do—I just work hard every day to keep healing and thrive ("not just survive," another Roberts gem).

I've lived most of my life fiercely protecting my vulnerabilities and weaknesses. I was a professional people pleaser and perfectionist by the age of six, which helped lead to my anorexia and depression. I was convinced my career would end if anybody found out about my abortion. Just thinking about the amount of energy I expended protecting my secrets exhausts me. But at least now I am free, and telling my story has changed my life forever, and I hope it can for you, too.

I could keep writing and editing this because I will never stop working to heal my narrative and make grand steps for my mental health. We all have the power to do this . . . but since I can't keep writing and rewriting this book, let's get started with something signature Ginger.

CHAPTER ONE
THE DRAIN

I was just coming out of a heavy sleep, my head felt swollen, and I was dizzy and dehydrated. When I licked my lips, I tasted the sour leftovers of the vomit I'd thrown up into the garbage can next to the bed. I rolled to my side and attempted to sit up, but a massive headache slammed me back to the pillow. I knew it was evening by the setting sun outside the window, and that was confusing. Hangovers were usually a morning thing at this juncture in my life. My left butt cheek hurt, and when I lifted the covers, I saw that I was naked.

I figured out that I was in my boyfriend Jacob's bedroom and started remembering how I got here. We woke up together this morning, probably about twelve hours ago, had coffee, and went to work. We both worked at a country club in Grand Rapids, Michigan. I was a waitress and Jacob worked in the athletic club. I loved that job and had been working there since I started busing tables when I was sixteen years old.

Around lunchtime, my boss, Cindi, invited me to join her with the wine representative and a few other employees in the private dining room. Cindi was no joke—a strict but loving woman who was serious about our work, the members, and making the club excellent from top to bottom. I'd been waiting for this invitation since my first day at work six years before. In that time, Cindi had taught me so much and I had climbed the ranks quickly from busing tables to now manager on duty. I was always adamant about making sure Cindi was pleased and that all rules were followed to a tee; my goody-two-shoes-ness had not worn off.

The wine representative held tasting classes with Cindi and a few of the senior waitstaff a few times a year in an effort to educate the managers about the wines that we would be serving in the coming months. I would enviously watch them all take off their waitressing belts, untuck their stained shirts from the morning and lunch rush, and relax into this elite club. I would usually keep working feverishly to show my dedication to the job, thinking someday I'd be in that room. I would slyly eavesdrop outside, or most fruitful were the moments Cindi waved me in to clear their glasses and snacks. While I leaned over the discarded goblets, my ears were alive. I'd memorized words like *smoky, red currant,* and *tannins,* trying to imagine the day I could taste these and have a true understanding of *terroir* (a French term used to describe the environmental factors that affect a crop of wine grapes).

I felt like Renée Zellweger in *Jerry Maguire* in the scene on the airplane when she tells her son, "First class is what's wrong, honey. It used to mean a better meal, now it means a better life."

Today I was being invited to sit in first class. I washed my hands in the bathroom and wished I had time to change my clothes. I unceremoniously ripped my server's belt off and, with pride, unbuttoned and untucked my shirt. The wine representative was dressed in all black: black pencil skirt, modest black heels, and a fitted black sweater with a string of pearls that were too big to be real. She had just finished pouring three small glasses of different white wines in front of the group when I slid into my seat. The table was a "round" that we used for eight or ten people at a wedding. Today it was barely adorned with a single white tablecloth in the middle of this meeting room that would be set later for the next day's Rotary Club meeting. Those guys loved a good Arnold Palmer (lemonade and iced tea). But no Arnold Palmers sat before us now—it was all chic wine. I kept staring at the wooden podium and Rotary flag when I felt uncomfortable.

The white wines tasted great. Refreshing, crisp . . . I kept rehearsing in case I was asked.

When the wine representative moved on to red, I was served a glass. I sipped it very, very slowly to give the impression that I was carefully considering its notes, but by this point I was happily thinking she'd avoid asking for the new girl's opinion. Luckily, I had a few words up my sleeve and took a shot when she looked at me.

"What do you taste, Ginger?"

"Smoky?"

Everyone in the room laughed except the wine representative, who generously let me off the hook.

"I think this one is more fruit forward, like a bowl of berries at the end, don't you?" she asked.

I nodded and we moved on. I started feeling the buzz deepen after my next tasting flight. I looked around as the room began to warm and blur. *Is everyone else feeling this toasty?* I wondered. Then I noticed Cindi's tasting glasses were still nearly full.

Ohhhh, I realized, *she's barely drinking. She's actually just tasting and moving on.* You would think that would have been one of the clues I picked up in my past detective-like observations of these events.

As soon as this realization came over me, the wine representative announced that she had something special she wanted to show us.

"This is a new mixer called Red Bull. It goes very well with vodka."

Cindi shook her head, pushing her chair away.

She was not interested in trying it, and I could tell she was not interested in allowing her employees to drink hard liquor in the middle of the day.

Her daughters, who were my coworkers, convinced her we would be fine.

"One sip," Cindi said as she reluctantly got up and turned back toward us, adding:

"You are all adults. You can make a decision for yourself."

She had obviously never tasted Red Bull.

The wine representative held up the blue-and-silver can that read *It gives you wings*. I took a sip. And then another. And after that moment the world sped up.

We proceeded to pour a shot of vodka and some Red Bull into a tall glass with ice cubes. I drank mine fast. It was sweet but not too sweet. It sipped so easily and masked any flavor of the vodka. If the wine representative had asked my opinion on this one, it would have been a lot easier. As well as it went down, it worked even more quickly. Being drunk always had a sleepy quality to it for me, but now I felt loose and sharp at the same time. I asked for another. And another. Red Bull didn't just give me wings, it transformed me into someone I wasn't. Wingless Ginger never would have broken the rules.

Pretty sure I'd downed three glasses of wine and three Red Bull vodkas by the time Jacob walked in.

I have no idea how he knew that I needed help, but it must have been his super-boyfriend Spidey sense. The tasting had digressed into a chatty gossip session so when Jake motioned for me to come meet him, I didn't think twice about it and bounded toward the door with the energy of a cheetah.

He led me into the storage room where he was hauling chairs from the last banquet. I offered him a taste of this delicious new drink, and he agreed that it was pretty good.

"You're wasted."

Jake wasn't judging me; he never did that. But he'd seen me get drunk before and do stupid things that I'd regret the next day, and now he was doing his best to prevent that from happening at work. He knew how much I respected Cindi and loved my job. He followed me back to the kitchen as I, slurring I am sure, promised him I was fine. A few minutes later, I stumbled over a tray stand. One of my fellow tasters that was "flying" was so gone she washed her hands under the boiling-hot water attached to the coffeemaker where we made hot tea. Before things got any uglier, Jake told me to get my things and helped me leave as discreetly as possible.

Jake and I retreated to the basement, and I was singing at the top of my lungs. Poor Jake, trying to hush and entertain me while keeping me away from the club members.

He gingerly ushered me into the supply closet and told me to stay there while he ran into the men's locker room to get his keys.

When he took more than thirty seconds, I began wandering into the downstairs kitchen that opened up to the bar. I've never stolen anything in my life, but I was "flying," so I grabbed a bottle of Cabernet from the wine rack. I could feel the caffeine from the Red Bull attaching to every blood vessel.

"Ginger—what are you doing?"

As I swung around to inform Jacob that we should keep the party going, I dropped the bottle on the floor, the glorious red liquid splattering all over the walls and my white tuxedo shirt. I bent down and did a big inhale:

"Mmmm, now that's smoky."

I laughed as I lunged for one of the big shards of glass to start cleaning up my mess, and sliced off a huge piece of my pinky.

"Uh-oh," I said coyly, looking up at Jacob. I held my bloody finger to my wine-splattered shirt, which now looked like I'd been knifed during a grape-stomping competition, but I barely felt it.

Jake wrapped my hand in a towel and told me to wait in the storage unit while he cleaned up the mess.

"I mean it—don't go anywhere."

I grabbed a can of Red Bull and another bottle of wine for the road, Jake pulling me along as I attempted to salsa dance all the way to the parking lot.

Jake was such a light in my life. We'd met at the same country club six years before this bloodied, inebriated afternoon. We were both sixteen and so excited to have our first jobs at "the club," as we called it. Jake, back then, worked as a dishwasher, and I was busing tables. I spent my time stacking plates, squatting to lift heavy trays, and constantly looking for reasons to go into the kitchen and stare into Jake's gentle blue eyes through the steam and racks of dirty dishes. I was dating Leo (my high-school boyfriend), so Jake and I never hooked up, but we did become great friends. We worked at the club each summer during college and flirted for the next four years, until this particular summer when we finally started dating. Jake was the kind of guy who looked out for his friends, and I always felt safe around him. He made every day feel like a celebration, and when I went too far, which was often, he just gave me that tender smile and helped me through.

By the time we got back to Jacob's house, I was a mess. I got undressed and flipped through his CDs because I wanted to have a dance party. I pulled the towel off my pinky while he went around the back of the house to turn on the shower for me. Suddenly I got really tired and lay down on his couch. The room was spinning, and I yelled out to Jake that I was feeling sick. But before he could make it back to me, I puked all over his CDs, his new rug, and the coffee table. He got me out of my clothes and practically carried me into the shower, where I threw up again. He situated me in the shower and the hot, steamy air took over. Jake shut the door and that's the last thing I remember.

"How are you feeling? Better than the hip-hop section of my CDs, I hope?"

That was Jake's next question now that I was awake from

my stupor. I loved that he could joke about it as he sat on the side of his bed lightly rubbing my head.

"Pretty rough," I answered.

He helped me sit up on the bed, and he wrapped his arms around me.

"I love you so much," he told me.

Why was he acting so worried? Even more to the point, why did he love somebody who got so stinking drunk and threw up in his house?

"I thought I was going to lose you."

I looked at my finger, which was now somehow neatly and mysteriously bandaged.

"Because of my finger?" I asked.

"Because you almost drowned, Ginger."

Apparently, when he'd left me to go clean up the vomit in the living room, I was standing up in the stall shower. But when he returned, I was sitting on the floor, and the water was filling up so quickly it was just about to cover my face. Jake threw the shower door open, and the water rushed out all over the bathroom floor. I poured out onto the floor with all the water, covered in my blood and vomit.

"Let me see your butt," Jake said.

I turned over so he could take a look.

"Yep, your butt stopped up the drain."

Sure enough, there were little indent marks on my rear

end that matched the shower drain. We both started laughing and crying, thinking about the headline DRUNK GIRL RESCUED FROM THE ARMS OF DEATH BEFORE HER BUTT STOPPED THE SHOWER DRAIN AND NEARLY ENDED IT ALL.

It's a funny (and not funny) story, but unfortunately it wasn't an isolated incident. I had enough drunken escapades in my twenties to know that it's only because I had people like Jake around me, who loved and looked out for me, that I made it out alive. I would never consider myself an alcoholic, because I know that is its own disease. The alcohol was my Band-Aid, not my disease. My disease was depression, and alcohol abuse is a common way of dealing with depression.

At least I learned some lessons from that wild and reckless night. For example, as popular as Red Bull and vodka became, I never touched it again and I never will.

CHAPTER TWO
It Really Doesn't Matter and Nobody Cares

I know. This sounds like a horrible thing for someone who has twice attempted suicide to say, but I've learned that it's actually the most powerful way to live.

I was recently being interviewed about my first book and the young journalist took great care in setting up her camera, making sure that my microphone was perfectly placed, and triple-checking the focus and white balance. She was obviously a little green and slightly nervous, but I found such joy in watching her process because it made me grateful. Her first question was one I've been asked before:

"What advice would you give to your younger self?"

You can imagine her surprise when I did not reply "Follow your dreams" or "Learn to say no" and instead gave her:

"It really doesn't matter and nobody cares."

When I think of the "younger self" I want to talk to, it's me at about ten years old. Not because I was finally in double digits, or because I was on the verge of puberty, but because ten was the age when I started to hate myself. It makes me sad that I have to go back so far and that the roots of my depression began this early. Dr. Wilson told me that the foundations of our personality are actually already in place by the age of seven, so it makes sense that by the age of ten I could have already been in distress. Our steps toward autonomy from our parents begin around ten, too.

Ten was right in the wake of my parents' divorce (they divorced when I was seven), the year that I was forced to switch schools, and the first time I really felt my life was out of control. My defense mechanisms included controlling my eating, which advanced into full-blown anorexia that year. At ten, the restricting began; by thirteen, I was in the deepest levels of the eating disorder; and throughout it all I had the emotional maturity of a kindergartner.

I have such a soft place in my heart for that ten-year-old little girl and her pudgy belly. With a little more self-compassion, some education, and perspective, all that baby fat would have just fallen off as I stretched up into a teenager.

But back to the answer to the young journalist's question. I would tell my younger self to open up and talk to people, to express her feelings, and learn to set and respect her boundaries. I would teach her about "the fence," a coping tool I came up with when I was hospitalized for depression and suicidal ideation at age thirty that allows me to set healthy boundaries and not absorb everyone's emotions around me. I would emphasize that she has value and that what she has to say matters to people. "Don't hold back, use your voice," I would tell her.

Then I would tell her it's not normal to have a ridiculous joint custody agreement where you have to pack up and move from Mom to Dad every Christmas and then do it all again from Dad to Mom at Easter. It is not healthy to never know consistency or structure. I would teach her ways to live with volatile parents and an ever-changing family structure; I would assure her that all the moves and school changes would one day make her stronger. I might also drop the knowledge that it's not normal to dislike snow days because you had to stay home from school, the one place you felt safe from it all.

I would show her how to meditate and teach her the value of cleansing your brain of negative, harmful thoughts. I would tell her to let her friends and family love her the way they want to because they are your support system in good times and bad. I would teach her appreciation and gratitude. And finally, I would tell her that none of it really matters and nobody cares.

Because it really doesn't. And they don't.

Think back right now to an instance where you couldn't sleep because you were worrying about something. Can you even remember why, what day it was, or the context?

Even when it's happening right now, most of what I build up in my head as a huge, dramatic, sleep-blocking event always works out. For example, six months after a major promotion at GMA to take over the weekday broadcasts, my bosses told me that I no longer fit at the new desk they had built. A week after that and without notice, my name was dropped from the opening credits. It felt like a horrible demotion, and I was sure it was the beginning of the end for me. But it turned out it wasn't personal. Nobody was going out of their way to hurt me, no one was laser pointing a scalpel at the show and cutting me out. My bosses were simply changing the show to focus on the three anchors. And I wasn't one of those three.

I remember losing a lot of sleep thinking, *How am I going to help support the child I have growing inside me?* (I was seven months pregnant when all this went down.) *Was it because I got pregnant? How will I get work?*

I then made the intelligent decision to utilize the people around me who have been in this longer than me. I asked George Stephanopoulos for a meeting. George is a kind man, doting father, and husband, but at work, he is all business. So I didn't really have the chummy relationship where I could just ease into his dressing room before the show and start asking questions. Plus, in morning TV, before the show just isn't an option. Time is limited. After the show, George rushes up to our other offices. So I asked for a formal meeting and plopped down on the chair across from him. Immediately I was so glad that I had come, and there he gave me some of the best advice I've ever received.

George told me that at least half a dozen times in his career something happened at work and he was sure he was about to be fired. In his case, sometimes even the newspapers and gossip columns were saying it was true. He got through it by reminding himself he was skilled and experienced at his job. He spent years educating himself to be a journalist, he had decades of experience in politics, and he knew he was good.

He told me I had every right to have the same confidence and promised that it would get me through my fear. And he was right—I'm a degreed meteorologist, a scientist, extremely hardworking, and an experienced storm chaser and storyteller. Most importantly, this change of show format that had kept me awake for weeks would not matter in the end. Because most things don't.

Keep your head down and do the job, because that's all you can control anyway.

Life is going to have its bumps, that's just reality. Taking George's advice to heart not only got me through the format change at work, but it has served me in my personal life as well. People are going to have their opinions about you and they're not always going to be great. They will be fickle and you can't change what others think of you. Nor should you want to. You should be unapologetically the best version of you that you can be. Be kind, fair, and decent, and don't worry about what other people think because it really doesn't matter.

And did I mention nobody cares?

Most of us lose the freedom of living the way we want as we go through childhood. I know that was the last time I felt like I spoke my truth, didn't care what others thought, and innocently lived a pure and joyful life.

I often describe it as the last time I was able to feel like "me" as a whole. Since I was about six I have instead always felt like I had two people inside me.

My middle name is Renee and I know this may seem strange, but I think of Renee as part of me and Ginger as the other part. You could look at it like the way Sasha Fierce is to Beyoncé. Not familiar? Beyoncé often describes her onstage persona as Sasha Fierce, a badass, confident, talented woman. She then describes her at-home, in-person persona as Beyoncé. So, my Renee versus Ginger feeling is like that without the global sensation, Queen Bey part.

The Ginger part of me is the outgoing, happy, fearless, boisterous little girl (now woman) who wanted nothing more than to be everyone's best friend on the playground. The girl who loved her teachers genuinely and was often accused of brown-nosing but was actually interested in everyone's lives. She truly fits my namesake—the movie star from *Gilligan's Island*. Ginger doesn't live by society's rules and absolutely marches to the beat of her own drum. Ginger would have tried more musical theater and pursued acting because that is genuinely what I wanted in my heart.

Renee is slower, more cautious. Painfully shy and almost sullen at times. What kind of kindergartner is sullen? Well, that part of me was and still is today. She wanted to sit in the back—Ginger prevailed and I sat in the front and fought Renee. She never wanted to raise her hand even though she knew the answer. I always did to spite her. You get the point. Instead of good and evil sitting on my shoulders, I had the extrovert and the introvert.

It was easier to steamroll her negativity when I was younger. But as time passed, environmental issues influenced me, cynicism entered, and the Renee voice grew louder and easier to follow.

Ginger and Renee had their first memorable battle when I was six years old. I begged my parents to put me in a classic jazz, ballet, and tap-dance class. I remember entering the class tentatively but with such hope and aspiration to do my best, to have a great time, and to meet new friends. But as soon as I walked through the doors, Renee saw the other girls prancing and stretching, and she tried to force me to turn around and leave. In my mind's eye, I saw Ginger reach for little Renee's hand and convince her to at least give it a try.

The class began with the teacher gathering all the little girls into a circle. We were supposed to go around the room and introduce ourselves, but when it was my turn, Renee was back in charge. My hands were clammy and my voice cracked. When the teacher asked me to speak up, I couldn't and the other girls started giggling.

Things went from bad to worse, so you can imagine it was no surprise to me when the teacher took my mom to the side afterward. They were both doing the thing where they were obviously talking about me as I waited with my coat over my leotard and tights. My mom glanced my way with a forced smile to make it seem like all was okay. Usually I wouldn't have paid any attention to this. Heck, usually this conversation wouldn't have been happening. But I had let Renee win. I was shirking the attention and being wrapped up in her concern of what others thought. She always worried about what my parents thought or what friends at school might say. I could usually tune Renee's voice out, but this was the first time I really felt her pulling at me. No matter how hard I fought it, I let it take over.

My mom didn't say anything for a few minutes, and I was too afraid to ask her what my teacher said about me. Finally she broke:

"How did you like the class?" she asked.

"I hate it," I said.

"*Hate* is a strong word, Ginger. You know we don't use that word."

"Well then, I really don't like it."

And then I started crying.

When I told her I didn't want to go back, she said fine. I guess I expected her to fight me on this. I probably wanted her to. I didn't want Renee to win. But Renee was certainly happy. The tights went in the closet and I went back to my comfort zone. Back to snacks and *Punky Brewster* after school. Safe again.

But life isn't about being safe. I knew that and the Ginger part of me wanted something else so I could prove that Renee was not going to rule my little life.

Then the advertisement came in the mail: Little Miss Junior America Pageant.

As soon as I got off the bus and ran inside, my mom was waiting for me with the flyer.

"Hi, Ging, how was school?"

"Great!" I exclaimed. Renee's voice hadn't dented my love of school.

"Would you like to be in a pageant?"

I had a brief return of the Renee voice that tried to edge in and say how I was not good enough, pretty enough.

I cut her off.

"Yeah!" I excitedly answered.

I didn't know exactly what a pageant was, but I didn't care. I was not going to let that Eeyore of a voice in my head stop me this time.

My mom had no experience with pageants, but she is a dreamer who thrives on passion, focus, and determination. If that's what I wanted, she was all in. She immediately got to work sewing me a blue satin dress after long twenty-four-hour shifts as a neonatal nurse practitioner. For all the negative volatile times, there were twice as many times my mom's volatility worked in our favor. She was unashamedly supportive even when it had no merit. My aim was to stay ahead of Renee so she had zero chance of winning this one.

When the day of the pageant arrived, I was nervous, but I just kept repeating a popular quote from a Disney attraction that was one of my mom's favorites: "If you can dream it, you can do it."

The pageant was held at a conference center, and it was full of little girls and their parents who also had a dream. I marched in with my parents and my blue satin dress casually draped over my arm like I'd been on the pageant circuit my entire life. Even though the other girls had fancy store-bought dresses, professionally styled hair and makeup, I was feeling myself. Ginger was in the house and she came to win.

In the first round, each girl was asked to walk up to the

microphone and answer questions from the panel. For this section I wore a snazzy green-and-black plaid skirt, white lace socks, Mary Janes, and a red wool blazer. It was the same exact outfit that I had worn in my family's one and only professional photo shoot about a year earlier. When they called my name, I did what I was supposed to, even though the lights were much brighter and hotter than I'd expected. Why was I wearing my coat when nobody else was? But there were no do-overs and I refocused. The emcee asked the first question.

"What city are you from?"

I tipped the mic toward me and answered. "Michigan."

Laughter erupted from the crowd. I tried to find my parents in the audience, but the lights were too bright. Why was my answer so funny?

"And what state are you from?"

"Grand Rapids," I answered.

The laughter got louder and I was even more confused. I stayed planted by the microphone for a moment until the next girl's name was called and then I went backstage. My parents hugged and kissed me and told me how well I did. Ginger was still the boss.

I made it through the interview round and the "athletic round," where we paraded on stage as a group in our pageant T-shirts and shorts.

The final round was evening gowns, and we were supposed

to hit different marks onstage. By the end of the show, I was full of sass and confident that I had a shot at winning. We stood in a line across the stage as the judges started by announcing the second runner-up. Phew. Not me. Someone else's name for the runner-up. I felt like a rocket just before *blastoff*. I brushed the front of my dress so I'd be ready to take my place center stage.

And then they called the winner—and it wasn't me.

My little jaw dropped in shock. I looked around at the other girls—two of them were crying. I waited for the audience to demand a recount. I wanted the sea of people to do something, anything, instead of clapping. I was flabbergasted. I couldn't even remember the winning girl's performance, and there she was, getting her photo taken holding a giant bouquet of flowers and wearing a shiny crown perched on her head. It was one of those movie-like moments where the roar of the clapping and the whistling crowd becomes a hum for me, and then silence.

The rest of us got certificates and participation trophies from the judges and went backstage to find our parents. I handed my trophy over to my dad and one of the plastic spikes on the crown broke off. I didn't care. Ginger was slipping away in defeat, ceding center stage once again to mopey Renee. My dad could see I was taking it all pretty hard and took his best shot.

"Let's get out of here. This place is cheap and the judges obviously don't know what they are talking about," he said.

My dad made me feel good for trying and my mom told me I would always be her "little winner." For a six-year-old, that was enough to bring Ginger back. Ginger just wanted to be loved. With their words of support, I wasn't even thinking about Renee.

Unfortunately, that would be the last time I felt 100 percent Ginger, and the last time *It really doesn't matter and nobody cares* came so easily and naturally. In between, she'd make an appearance now and then, but it was more like a cameo than a leading role.

There is nothing a child wants more than the love and approval of their parents. This is the last time I can remember them ever sharing those feelings for me. I know that this was a pivotal point in my evolving sense of self-worth. These days, when I read books and visit websites about being the best parent I can be, one thing stands out: we give our children their voices in the beginning. This was the last time I was given support in finding that inner voice. After my parents' divorce, it was mostly up to me and I did not do well.

A solid twenty years of allowing Renee to rule was finally broken by therapy. Therapy gave me tools that I didn't have as a kid. Not too unlike the "Daily Affirmations" with Stuart Smalley on *Saturday Night Live*, where the character stares in the mirror and says, "I am good enough, smart enough, and gosh darn it, people like me." I learned to give myself pep talks to get ahead of any possible fears or insecurities that might coax Renee out of hiding. Early in my career, right before I'd go on air, I started saying to myself, then saying with my eyes, *People want this information, you are worthy of people's attention, you are valuable.* That helped thwart jitters and combat the common verbal assaults I might have been served by viewers or bosses, but I really believe it helped me be confident and convey my message clearly.

When I face the camera even today, I try to focus my intentions on what I want people to know about me or my report. You can believe me, I'm credible, I know what I'm talking about, and it sends the energy in the right direction and establishes a connection with my audience.

At the age of twenty-three, I had my second on-air job as a meteorologist in Grand Rapids. I knew I had a lot to learn and that my performance needed improvement. I hadn't taken any communications or broadcasting classes, and although I'd been told by my professors and bosses that I had "it," I also knew that my "it" needed some polishing. I signed up for voice lessons and improv class and my confidence grew. When I moved to Chicago, I took an acting class at Second City, and recently I picked back up with both voice and acting classes. I'm a big fan of continuing education and growth in both my personal and professional lives, plus the classes are a lot of fun.

My husband gifted me acting lessons a few years ago and my acting coach, Bridget Berger, helped me reclaim the voice I lost. As soon as she met me, she shared with me that my fire chakra was covered. I learned that the fire chakra resides above the navel because it's the origin of your personal power, self-worth, and will power—and ultimately your voice.

My teacher observed that my fire chakra opened up onstage when I was in character. But my fire chakra shut down as soon as I went back to being me. This was a revelation for me, but it made perfect sense. On TV, I have developed a strong, confident character that embodies Ginger. In life, I am still letting Renee win. Because I'm so soft-spoken, people sometimes tell me that I'm hard to hear. When my husband, who is naturally loud, edits a video that we've done together, he has to boost my audio more than anyone he's ever worked with.

My voice coach, Natalie Tyson-Multhaup, has been helping me find where projection comes from. While much of it can be based on an individual's facial structure and diaphragm strength, projection is also developed over time. My childhood insecurities impacted my ability to project my voice—but it's getting louder and stronger. Now I can tell when my fire chakra is open and I pair it with a forward speaking voice. People are seeing and hearing me for the first time.

I want to command, not to have to demand respect. Whether it's with my title (weather girl versus chief meteorologist) or with a colleague, I want to be a yes person with boundaries and make that clear for everyone else so there is never any confusion. I need to get that fire chakra working at all times.

I'm a work in progress, and that's okay.

And that's why I'm going to allow myself to make an addendum to that last line of advice to my younger self.

Nobody cares, but you have to make them when you want them to.

CHAPTER THREE
DIVORCE

I t's not your fault.

Almost every parent who's going through a divorce, including mine, wants their kids to believe this, but it doesn't always work. It's normal for a kid to internalize the blame because it's usually the way they can make sense of it. In my case, I blamed myself before I was even born.

My parents got married because my mom was pregnant with me. They had been dating on and off for a year when my mom found out, but it wasn't a case of *Well, we're in love and this is a good reason to not wait and get married now.*

My mom had been told she wasn't going to be able to have children because of endometriosis, so getting pregnant was a miracle she couldn't count on happening again. My mom wanted to be a neonatal nurse practitioner, and while I think she hoped my dad would say he was along for the adventure, I know she would have done it without him. My dad was so surprised, but as my mom describes it, surprisingly elated to become a father. So they got married.

I don't know if it's the powder-blue tuxedo my dad is wearing or the perfect afternoon light reflecting off my mom's raven hair, but when I look at their wedding photo, I see happiness. Maybe it was naïveté. Either way, it's a sentiment or look I often craved to see repeated in them but wouldn't.

They moved to California just before I was born because my mom had already planned to get her master's in nursing out there before the whole pregnancy shock. My dad looked after me every day while my mom went to classes. My mom tells me she would pull up to their little apartment in Orange, California, and he would be holding me right up to the screen of the window screaming; I was ready for food. She would run in and nurse me. My dad tells me he would take me to the local high-school track, put me in the middle in my bassinet stroller, and then he would run quarter miles around, checking on me every lap.

Part of me wondered if their blissfulness would have been prolonged had we not moved away from the warmth and sunshine of Southern California.

But once my mom had her degree, they moved back to West Michigan. My mom did get pregnant again with my brother, Sean, and my dad started a business building tennis courts. I was about five when I first noticed how bad things were between him and my mom.

We had just moved to our brand-new construction, their dream home. We called it Foxfire for the lane it was built on. It was a modern, 1980s loft-style house with high ceilings, a wood-burning fireplace, geothermal heating, and had everything a house off the grid in the woods should have.

There was carpet in the living room underneath flower pots filled with lipstick plants. Those lipstick flowers were so beautiful, but they fell and made a mess every so often. My dad would vacuum and I remember my mom being pleased when he would do that. My mom was always happy when everyone was being productive and doing something for the greater family good.

Aside from vacuuming that living room, my dad was good at relaxing. My mom is not good at relaxing. That seemingly small difference in two people exacerbated tensions over and over again the first year we lived at Foxfire.

It wasn't just about my dad relaxing. My mom wanted a more involved partner who was less critical and more loving. My dad was resentful of her volatility, which was often fueled by the long hours she spent working at the hospital. It was a complicated relationship.

Sometimes opposites attract, but with my parents, I think they just brought out the worst in each other. My mom needed someone who could be extremely patient, but most of all needed someone who could communicate their love. Or could just communicate in general. For a myriad of reasons, my dad wasn't that guy.

They were constantly fighting and snapping at each other. I cannot remember ever seeing my parents acting civil to each other, much less loving. The most my brother and I could hope for was that they'd give each other the silent treatment.

But little did we know that after the divorce the silent treatment would last twelve years. My brother and I were relegated to the role of middlemen, tasked with sending messages back and forth across enemy lines.

"Mom, I need twenty-five dollars for a new cheerleading bodysuit."

"Go ask your father."

"Dad, I need twenty-five dollars for a new bodysuit for cheerleading."

"What's wrong with the old one? You want it, go ask your mother."

Instead of going back across enemy lines, I chose a more self-reliant solution: I colored the skin of my shoulder with mascara so when I put the bodysuit over it you could barely tell there was a growing hole.

It was exhausting being the ball in the world's longest, nastiest tennis match. Sometimes it worked out, but I'd stress and worry about it, until one of my parents gave in at the last minute. Then there'd be another issue and the process would start all over again. Not to mention the poor girl who I hoisted up during our cheer competition ended up looking like she had a big bruise on her leg from the mascara on my shoulder. It wasn't fair to anyone.

My mom got remarried to a man named Carl three years after the divorce. He is a social worker and the perfect person to communicate with my mom. They bought a farm and moved to the nearby town of Belmont. My dad had a new nickname for my mom that he used anytime my mom would call while we were staying with him.

"Kids! The witch from the farm is on the phone!" It's not the best-written joke, but Sean and I laughed because we were kids, and I'm sure that just encouraged my dad to keep being ugly to her.

My mom had her own way with words she lobbed back at my dad.

"Is your father going to pay for camp?"

"I don't know."

"He's such a fucking derelict."

My mom was smart and she had a great vocabulary. She was a particular fan of the word *derelict* to describe my dad. I didn't know what it meant, but I knew it wasn't a compliment.

The first Christmas after the divorce, my brother and I saw almost as many cities as a touring rock band. First, we drove to Chicago with my mom and Carl so we could meet his family. Then Sean and I flew by ourselves to Montana to meet my dad's new wife Pam's family. After that we went to visit my mom's sister in Palm Springs. Our final stop on the "1987 Kids of Divorce Holiday Tour" was in Fort Lauderdale to see my dad's sister.

By the end of our vacation, Sean and I were exhausted. We came home with a haul of Christmas gifts bigger than any we'd had when our parents were married. We even came home with cash. Somehow even our parents' relatives knew there was a fierce competition going on for which parent we loved more.

There's a photo taken that Christmas that perfectly captures the effect this competition had on me. My hair is crimped because it's the 1980s and I'm a little too tan because . . . well, it's the 1980s. My tan little ankle is wrapped in my new ankle bracelets, and I'm sitting on my bed with a wad of cash between my lips like I'm starring in a preteen version of *Indecent Proposal*. Not exactly a picture of a little girl sitting on her shiny new pink bike with a big bow under the tree. When I look at the photo now I see sadness in my eyes. I didn't need all those things. I needed one home, one family.

It's not entirely my parents' fault, though. This was way before "uncoupling" (thank you, Gwyneth Paltrow). People didn't really talk about divorce, much less get any counseling on how to help their kids get through it.

The friends I have who are divorced are so thoughtful

with their children. Their goal is to present a unified front and keep the lines of communication open, leaving their kids free to just be kids. Divorce will never be easy, but when the kids come before whatever residual anger the grown-ups may have toward each other, there's a greater chance that the kids will come through it feeling loved and safe. When they watch their parents' civility and respect, they form healthy role models of relationships that aren't limited to people who stay together. They form a healthy base for identity. Something I did not have.

My parents didn't get any counseling, but they did try putting Sean and me in therapy for a few months. The therapist asked us to draw pictures of our family and talk about how Mom and Dad still loved us. But all we wanted was to hear it from them. It was a long ten years to live in the lawlessness that was my childhood. One of the many reasons I was thrilled to leave for college at Valparaiso University.

During my freshman year, an unexpected turn of events changed my family's dynamic. It was a Friday night and I was coming home from the gym when I saw a note from my roommate written on the eraser board in our room.

Call home immediately.

My heart fell to the bottom of my stomach. Who died and which home was I supposed to call? I called my mom first and the answering machine picked up. Dammit. I needed a person, not a machine. A few seconds later, that yellow phone on the wall of my dorm room rang with the most aggressive BRRRRING—it was my stepfather, Carl.

"Sean was in an accident."

My knees got so weak that I stumbled away from the phone, stretching the cord, and started crying.

"He's in surgery right now. It happened during a football game. Another kid's helmet went right through his leg and broke both bones under the knee. He's going to be okay, Ginger. I promise."

Carl was so calm I believed him. I finally took a breath.

"The doctor says he'll have to be in a wheelchair for a few months, but he should be able to walk again next spring."

And then he paused. There was something else he wanted to say.

"Are you sitting down?"

If you've ever watched television or seen a movie, you know something bad always follows this question.

"Your mom and dad talked."

I didn't just sit down, I fell down. Under normal circumstances, it would have been great news that after twelve years, the stalemate had been broken, but I'd given up long ago believing that they'd ever say a word to each other. My whole body went numb. I couldn't think, I couldn't feel, I couldn't breathe. Carl stayed on the phone while I finally had to take a breath to survive, and that opened the seal for the heaving to begin. The type of heaving cries that should be reserved for death.

My roommate Kirsten came back and hovered in our doorway watching me until I quieted enough to see her and nod that it was okay to come in. She held my hand and took the phone.

"Don't worry, I'll take care of her."

After hanging up with Carl, she gently asked me what happened.

"My brother is in surgery."

I choked on the next part.

"And my parents . . . talked to each other."

Saying it out loud was followed by me falling onto my bed and curling up in the fetal position. Kirsten had no way of knowing what a big deal this was, but she sat on the edge of my bed and listened as I explained.

I had come to accept that one day I'd get married and my husband and I would have to seat my parents at opposite sides of the reception. I often dreamed of becoming a mother, but that dream always had the attached fear that only one of my parents would be able to be at the hospital to meet their grandchild. I just tolerated all of it as our family baseline and now there was hope that things could be better. That things could be "normal." Because until even my freshman year of college, I think I was severely underdeveloped mentally and emotionally and never understood that "normal" or "ideal" was almost never possible. I wanted my parents to be together only because I wanted what I thought I saw in some of my friends' parents. I wanted them to love me. I wanted them to not judge each other. I needed them to love each other, and above all love me and Sean.

Thankfully, my brother came out of the accident okay. He knew he'd never play football again, but he picked up a guitar while he was recovering in a wheelchair and discovered he had a gift for music. He had a fantastic ear for it and a beautiful voice. About a year after the accident, he formed a band called Outer Vibe with his best friend, Nick. Music became my brother's path in life, and the band is still together today.

Sean's accident didn't just instigate the beginning of the change between my mom and dad, it solidified it. They went to every one of Outer Vibe's shows, and a few years in, they sat together with their new families. If you catch them today, you may even see them dancing together. They had Sean in common, and it was obvious how proud they were of him. They even take yoga together, with Carl, at the local YMCA. I might go so far as to call them all friends. The best part is that they sat next to each other at my wedding, and they were both in my hospital room when my first son was born.

The moment I realized I was beginning to heal and fully accept the type of family I have was during one of Sean's shows at the annual "Start of Summer" event in our home-town of Rockford. Outer Vibe was playing at the pavilion, and my parents, their spouses, and my two half sisters were listen-ing to Sean sing onstage. My six-year-old half sister, Elaina (my mom and Carl's daughter), turned to the girl sitting next to her.

"My brother's in the band."

Elaina had no idea that the girl she was talking to was my sixteen-year-old half sister, Bridget (my dad and Pam's daugh-ter), who responded: "My brother's in the band, too!"

"Well, my brother is the lead singer!"

Bridget giggled. "My brother's the lead singer, too!"

Elaina's bright blue eyes started to twinkle. She'd figured out how they both had a brother who was the lead singer.

"Are we . . . sisters?!"

"Kinda, yeah."

Elaina was too young to remember that she'd met Bridget before and figured it out on her own. We all had started to figure it out. This was our family, and I started realizing I was pretty darn lucky to have it—even if it wasn't what I felt was "normal."

It was a magical night, but it didn't erase my childhood. I still had a lot of issues and damage to work through in ther-apy, but this was my first step to moving forward with my life.

It's hard not to wonder what my life would have been like

if I'd had a "normal" childhood. Who would I have become if my parents had loved each other and stayed married? There's no way of knowing, of course, but my best friend, Brad (who you'll remember from chapter seven of my first book, *Natural Disaster*), has a theory that my success is driven by the love I didn't get from my parents. He thinks he would have been even more successful and driven (he is actually both) if his parents hadn't loved each other and him so much.

I don't know if I agree, but there's no harm in seeing my childhood in a positive light. But for my own family I want something different than what I had. I want my kids and my husband to know every single day how much I love and appreciate them. I want my boys to grow up and find their motivation and their path within themselves, knowing they have a family cheering them on every step of the way.

There's no question that my pattern of dysfunctional, sometimes dangerous relationships with men can, in part, be traced back to my parents' bitter dynamic. For most of my twenties, my comfort zone was men who would offer me the chaos that felt familiar to me, that felt like what I deserved.

But as I have learned in writing this book, I used to put far too much emphasis on my parents' divorce when in reality, there were other factors that would instigate a mental-health spiral that went far deeper than a simple divorce.

CHAPTER FOUR

PAM

There are several film titles that relate to parts of my life, but none so much as the 1980s classic *My Stepmother Is an Alien*. If you haven't seen it, Dan Aykroyd plays a widowed astronomer who accidentally disrupts an unknown planet's gravity. That planet is the home of an alien played by Kim Basinger. She is sent to Earth as a blond bombshell to figure out how to remedy her planet's gravity problem. Not only did my stepmother resemble Kim, but I would often find myself wondering if she was, indeed, from another planet.

In a child's mind, the universe is very small, containing home, school, family, and friends. As a result, anything outside that orbit can feel as far away as the moon.

My universe had already been disrupted by the divorce, but the day I met my stepmom, Pam, was the day that sent everything into the next galaxy. It was a pristine West Michigan summer day. My dad drove Sean and me in his brand-new red Corvette with red interior (note to Dad: not at all a middle-aged, divorced-guy cliché) out to Lake Michigan for an afternoon on his business partner's boat. We went fishing using corn and cheese as bait, we swam in the chilly water, and had fun throwing pieces of bread to the birds on the docks. On the way home, my dad suggested we stop for dinner at the Bil-Mar, a beachfront restaurant in Grand Haven State Park.

We got a table on the deck outside, overlooking Lake Michigan. This was the type of spontaneous fun my dad had started being known for post-divorce. We were sandy, happy, and starved, so my dad let us order chocolate milk *and* a Shirley Temple each. Thanks to my dad's divorce guilt, I not only had more sugar than ever before, but also more Barbies than all my friends put together, and I'd brought them with me to the Bil-Mar in a pink suitcase. When my dad's new girlfriend, Pam, showed up, I was so focused on Skipper and Classic Barbie's playdate that my dad had to tap me on the shoulder to look up. I caught my breath and my jaw fell open. The woman standing next to me was so beautiful I thought I must have wished my Barbie into a real person. I looked at my dad, and he seemed pretty impressed as well.

"Ging, Sean, this is my friend Pam."

In case your parents never got divorced, *friend* is divorced-parent code for *somebody I'm romantically interested in but don't*

want you and your mother to know about yet. But I knew. It
was obvious by the way he was looking at her, plus she was
gorgeous! Pam wasn't that tall, but she was statuesque. The
first time I met her she was wearing a bright yellow bikini and
cutoff jean shorts. She had a thick mane of strawberry-blond
hair that was feathered like Farrah Fawcett and tousled over
her tanned shoulders. Each freckle that ran across her cheeks
and nose looked as if God had placed it there like a price-
less painting. If she wasn't a real-life Barbie, she must've been
an alien.

Pam had a lot of alien qualities beyond her looks. She
talked to Sean and me like we were real people instead of
dumb little kids. My dad was clearly under the force of her
space powers—I'd never seen him flirt with my mom or any
woman before. He even agreed to her suggestion that we stop
at McDonald's for soft-serve ice cream. The way she ate ice
cream was unique—slowly but without a drop melting off the
cone. When my dad dropped us off, I said good-bye to Pam
and couldn't wait to see her again and learn more of her for-
eign ways. She was like a ravishing E.T. I ran into the house
to tell my mom all about Dad's new friend.

But it's hard to describe an alien to another earthling,
and my mom just didn't seem that interested. If only my mom
could meet Pam, she'd get it, I thought . . . but obviously that
was never going to happen since my mom and dad hadn't

spoken a word to each other since the divorce. It must have been torture for my mom to hear about her daughter's infatuation with her ex-husband's first new (and delightful) girlfriend who looked like Barbie.

Obviously, Pam was not a real alien, but she was from far, far away (at least in my little world). Most of the people I interacted with had been born, raised, and stayed in West Michigan. If anything, they had ventured to Chicago or Detroit and back, but not beyond that radius. Pam was born way outside that world, in Arlee, Montana, and went to college at Montana State University and medical school at the University of New Mexico (yes, I waited to mention that Pam is also a doctor!). When she started dating my dad, she was doing her ophthalmology residency in Grand Rapids and she was twenty-nine years old. On paper my dad didn't seem like an obvious choice for a stunning doctor: He was ten years older, recently divorced, with two kids, child support payments, and a small business. But they both loved tennis, cocktails, and boating and enjoyed each other's company. If Pam was Barbie, then my dad was Ken, and that was fine by me.

That first summer, Pam started coming to my dad's house on Dean Lake almost every weekend. I am sure she was there a lot more, but I was only there every other weekend so I wouldn't have known how close they were getting. What I did know was that I liked to ride the wave runners with Pam because she was more sensitive and cautious than my dad. My dad would whip us around doing donuts until we fell off, while Pam would allow for a gentle, serene ride.

Pam loved to go jogging in the morning and then sit out on the deck in her bikini to catch the sun rays. She always made sure to be through with her run by 11 a.m. because "that's when the strongest rays started." I'd stare at her from the billiards room through the screen door and try to gather up the courage to go outside and sit with her. I was nine with brown curly hair and relatively pale skin. I definitely did not have a suntanning game.

One day I had a great idea for a conversation starter. I dressed up all my Barbies in swimsuits and brought them outside in a Tupperware tub. Pam asked what I was doing.

"They're having a pool party."

"Sounds like a perfect afternoon to me!"

I loved that she didn't think I was a baby for playing with Barbies. This was going swimmingly. I now had an activity that didn't involve lying on a towel like a plank of wood yet gave me proximity to study Pam.

"How about you take a pool party break and join me inside for a cold glass of water? It's so hot out here."

Was she kidding? I would have ended that pool party by kicking my Barbies into the lake if she asked me to.

Inside the kitchen, Pam poured us each a glass of water.

I made sure to drink mine as slowly and carefully as she did. I wanted to adopt her exotic ways. Then she reached up to the top shelf in the cabinet and grabbed a plastic bag.

I wanted to remember everything about this moment: the cool inside air, the smell of suntan lotion, the sound of the ice cubes as the glass of water shook in my hand, and the way she untied the twist ties without ripping the bag like I did.

The bag was full of sugar-coated orange gummy slices that I knew had to be Pam's because my dad was against sugar aside from the occasional peanut M&M, because those had protein in them. This was her secret stash and she was sharing them with me.

"Don't tell your dad," she said with a wink.

I nodded and held the glorious gelatin candy under my tongue, determined to make it last forever. Pam, however, did not eat these candies like she ate her ice cream or drank her water. One by one she tossed them into her mouth and encouraged me to do the same. We didn't try to save any for Sean or my dad. It was heavenly.

The more time I spent with my new alien friend, the more I liked her. She baked M&M cookies for my fifth-grade Election Day, and I even started riding my bike next to her during some of her morning jogs. By December, my dad and Pam announced their engagement. I guess a lot of kids have problems when their parents get remarried, but I'd grown pretty close to my alien and now she'd be staying on our planet forever, which made me very happy.

They had a small but beautiful wedding at the Big Sky Resort in Montana. My brother and I dressed in black-and-white velvet and satin. Pam was ethereal in her wedding gown, and my dad looked stunningly handsome. Everything was punctuated by red rose petals, and bouquets of red roses framed us in our new family picture.

Instead of them taking a honeymoon, we all went skiing together and had a great time. The mornings were full of ski lessons on the giant northern Rockies, and the evenings were for hot chocolate around the fire and telling stories with Pam's parents, sisters, and their kids. No longer an alien, Pam was officially a part of our family.

Per the custody agreement, Sean and I moved in with my dad and Pam at Christmas. It must have been hard for Pam as a newlywed—suddenly there were two kids around with all kinds of needs and demands that took my dad's time and attention away from her. We weren't the only ones adapting.

In *My Stepmother Is an Alien*, Alyson Hannigan plays the daughter, and she suspects her new stepmother is an alien the whole time, but doesn't confirm it until she sees Kim Basinger eating the acid out of batteries and pulling hard-boiled eggs out of boiling water with her bare hands.

Here's where I had one of my closest parallels. One winter

afternoon, snow blowing for the third month in a row (West Michigan winters can get pretty gray and dreary thanks to the lake effect snow), I trotted down from my room, where I had been watching *Hey Dude* on Nickelodeon, to grab a snack and see what everyone else was doing. From the bottom of the stairs you could peer right past the dining room and into the kitchen. There, I saw Pam standing over the kitchen sink, her beautiful jaw opening wide, her perfectly straight teeth ready to gnash into a giant app— *Wait a minute.* I squinted my eyes. *That is either a very round purple apple or . . . oh my goodness, that woman is eating a red onion.* I stood there at the bottom of the stairs with my brow furrowed, staring, trying to make sense of what I was seeing. Unlike Alyson Hannigan's character, who kept it secret for a bit, I couldn't hold back. I blurted out:

"What in the world are you doing? That is so weird!"

I was chuckling until I saw the look she gave me. The late-winter-afternoon light was shining through the window, so she was backlit and I couldn't quite see how unhappy she was until I heard her response and tone.

She snapped back: "*Weird* is *not* a nice word. Apologize, then go to your room."

I apologized and shuffled up the steps toward my room. When I was halfway up the stairs, I turned around and took a few steps back down to say something else because I felt terrible. I hated getting in trouble for any reason, but this was the first time my adopted alien had used a sour tone with me. That's what had made her so special. She was the nice one, the one who didn't fight; she was supposed to make our planet friendly and sweet.

I stopped my apology from crossing my lips when I saw Pam just staring out the kitchen window. Any hurt I felt from her quick retort was replaced by empathy. Maybe she was regretting coming to our planet, and now she was trying desperately to figure out a way to get home. She still seemed happy around my dad, so if she left, it would definitely be my fault, I figured. I could survive, but I didn't want to be responsible for making my dad unhappy, so I vowed to be easier, quieter, and less judgmental. If she folded the towels in a way I had never seen or could re-create, or forgot I didn't like too much tomato sauce on my spaghetti, I'd bite my lip. But I had to face it: Pam was still an alien, and the more time I spent with her, the more it was apparent that we were not from the same place and the acclimation was going to take a lot longer than I expected.

Just before I started eighth grade, my dad and Pam announced that she was pregnant. I was so excited about having another brother or sister to play with and even more joyful when I saw how happy Pam seemed again. I didn't worry that my dad would no longer have time for me, or that he might decide he liked his new family better than his old one. All I thought about was how great it was that the baby was due in February because I was always at the house then and would be able to welcome the baby home.

And then one day when we were supposed to get picked up from school by my dad or Pam, my mom showed up instead. We learned that Pam had been in a bad car accident, and the doctors said it was because she had a seizure caused by a golf-ball-size tumor in her brain. Because she was pregnant, they couldn't operate, so as the winter months passed, we all just waited and prayed. None of us really knew what to expect. Four months later Pam gave birth to a healthy baby girl named Bridget Gabrielle. The doctors operated on Pam's brain the day after she gave birth and discovered the tumor was cancerous and had grown to the size of a softball.

Almost a week after the terrifying news, I finally got to see Pam and meet my baby sister. My dad's house back then was a trilevel, and the front room, which had been a formal sitting room, was now transformed into a nursery. As I turned the corner from the kitchen, fear swept over me.

I could hear Pam mumbling to my oma and the baby, then she lifted her head up and with pain in her smile said, "Hi, kids."

From a distance, Pam still looked exquisite. Her blond hair draped over her face as she situated the baby on her chest and rocked her back and forth. But as I got closer, I could see that Pam's beautiful strawberry-blond hair was matted to her skull, and her scalp was stapled from ear to ear like construction paper in a school project. I tried not to stare at the gaping wounds across her skull and decided it was easier to focus on the baby. Pristine skin, bright blond wisps of hair, and the most dazzling big blue eyes peered over the edge of the blanket.

"She's so cute," I exclaimed to Pam.

In that moment I caught her eye, she smiled in spite of her pain and exhaustion, and her warmth helped all my sadness and unease melt away.

But that warmth wouldn't be enough to kick the cancer from her brain forever. Pam and my dad decided to try a holistic alternative to chemotherapy in Tijuana, Mexico. My dad thought it would be nice to turn it into a family vacation. The plan was that we would drop Pam off at her treatment facility and then my dad, Sean, Bridget, Oma, and I would go to Southern California for a few days and then come back to pick her up when her treatment was finished.

Tijuana was the most depressing place I had ever seen. There were so many homeless people and the streets were dotted with broken-down shanties. Then, in a striking juxtaposition, the treatment facility appeared—a gleaming marble complex behind a heavily secured gate, and once you went through the gate, you could almost convince yourself it was a high-end vacation resort.

We waited with Pam to get her first IV treatment, and I saw a young boy who couldn't have been any older than Sean laid out on a stretcher with an IV in his arm. He was pale and looked too sick to even sit up. A nurse saw me staring and told me that the boy had leukemia. I had no idea what that was but assumed it was something maybe even worse than Pam's cancer.

It seems strange and downright wrong when I think about it now. Why didn't we stay with Pam? Why wouldn't we have brought another family member to take us all up to Los Angeles so my dad could at least stay with her. Or her sisters? Or parents?

Once she got settled in, we drove back up to Los Angeles. My brother and I were excited to see Universal Studios, and in my child-minded naïveté, I just hoped that Pam would be magically better when we returned.

The first day at Universal Studios, my dad, Oma, Sean, and I were backstage watching TLC film a video for their song "Waterfalls," when I got a terrible and sudden stomachache. I ran as fast as I could to the nearest ladies' room and discovered that I'd finally gotten my period. I was fourteen and the last one of my friends to get it. I always imagined my mom would be with me when it happened and would tell me what to do.

There was no way I was sharing this news with my father, so I decided to find Oma and ask her for a quarter for a "gum-ball" so I could buy a tampon from the machine in the bathroom. I had heard plenty of my friends throw the word *tampon* around, so I figured it wouldn't be too difficult to use. However, as soon as I tore off the paper and stared at the huge cardboard cylinder filled with cotton, I realized I really didn't know how to insert it correctly. It looked so big! I grabbed another quarter from my grandma and ran back to the bathroom for a giant maxi pad, which was the alternative.

I was uncomfortable with the diaper-like pad and my stomach still hurt, but I kept it all to myself as we walked through the park. When we rode the *Jaws* ride, I kept telling God I was grateful that this was a fake shark who wouldn't smell my blood and eat us all. (Note: After swimming with sharks on several occasions, I can promise they are repelled by human blood. I even watched a girl get bitten by a shark; sharks scattered once the blood was in the water. Another story for another time.)

I called my mom as soon as we got back, but she wasn't home. Thankfully, Pam called to talk to my dad, and I begged to talk to her. I curled up on the floor by the side of the motel bed, and as quietly as I could, I told her my big secret. She had a natural maternal instinct, and comforted me and told me this was a special day.

I hugged her so hard as soon as we got back to Tijuana

to pick her up. As we left, I saw that same boy who had been laid out with leukemia playing basketball with a staff member. Pam seemed to be in great spirits and health, too. This place was awesome.

And sure enough, Pam's treatment in Tijuana was successful and the doctors pronounced her officially "cancer-free" a few weeks after we returned to Michigan. We moved back to my mom's house at Easter.

Throughout that first year of Bridget's life, visits were good at my dad's. I even got to babysit Bridget all by myself several times. Pam got pregnant again just over a year later; my mom and Carl had just welcomed my other little sister, Adrianna. There were babies at both houses and now we were expecting a third new sibling in the span of less than three years.

These new aliens we were living with sure were prolific procreators.

This second pregnancy for Pam was lighter, more exciting, because as we watched her belly grow and considered baby names, there was no worry about cancer or tumors.

That next May, Walter was born and it was impossible not to notice that Pam had evolved into a mama bear, loving, protective, and available. My dad's new business, Racquet Sports, was booming and he wasn't around as much as before. I tried not to be jealous that Pam didn't treat Sean and me the same way she treated her own kids, but I was fifteen, so hormones were erratic and life was just difficult. Even with my teen attitude I didn't want to cause trouble, so I kept telling myself none of it mattered. But the night my dad forgot to pick me up from a volleyball game, it did matter. I waited and waited until well after it was dark before I called him on a pay phone.

"Where are you, Dad?"

"Shoot, you already played?"

"Two hours ago. Can you please come get me?"

"Yeah, just gotta get the kids to bed."

And that's when I had to face the facts. My dad had a new family, my mom had a new family, and those families came first.

Fast-forward to the following winter, the winter of my sophomore year. My high school had an annual Swirl Dance where the girls had to ask the boys. I asked Leo, who was my new boyfriend, and I was a little nervous because we hadn't ever danced together, let alone kissed much, and I was sure a lot of both of these things were going to happen that night.

I was getting ready at my dad's house when my friend Lindsey called and asked if she could borrow my corset bra. I said of course. Lindsey was too busy getting her hair done for the dance, so her mom came to pick it up instead. As soon as she rang the doorbell, baby Walter woke from a deep sleep and started screaming. The kind of screaming that shakes the floors of the house. Pam ran down the stairs and shot me a deadly look.

"Who in the world is this?! Is this for you?"

I had no idea this would happen, but Pam was getting frustrated with me a lot that winter. She said Sean and I were "difficult" and she didn't look at us with the same warmth that she once had. Even when she didn't say it, she said it with her eyes. The division between her family and whatever we were at this point was clear.

I resented that my dad didn't notice any of this. I was done being quiet, pretending it was okay that Pam's babies came first, and mostly I was done with my crush on Pam as our honeymoon was officially over.

Pam asked Lindsey's mother to come inside. Maybe Lindsey's mom heard Pam snapping at me and would stick up for me. She didn't. Pam made friendly small talk with the woman as if they were best friends who were going to have afternoon tea together.

I ran up to my room, and when Lindsey's mom left, Pam quietly knocked on the door.

Everything she did was usually quiet, gentle, deliberate.

But not this time.

"What were you thinking? Now I won't be able to get the baby back to sleep! I'm exhausted! I can't do this anymore. Something needs to change! Every winter when you two move in, it rocks this house and disturbs *our* home."

"I'm sorry," I muttered quietly, and she just slammed the door and left. I heard that last part more clearly than I'd felt any of the death stares I had felt before. This was not *my* home. She meant *their* home. That did not include Sean and me.

No matter the disagreement (even the red onion moment), Pam had never raised her voice to me like that. Her anger in the past had been passive-aggressive, but this was the breaking point.

So there I was, crying on my bed, with just a few hours until my high-school dance with my first long-term boyfriend, who was going to give me my first big kiss. My beautiful silver velvet dress with a fish-scale-like design was still hanging in my closet with my new strappy heels, but I didn't care. Pam had ruined everything in my teenage mind. She'd fooled me into thinking she was a friendly alien. Barbie would never yell like that. I sat and stewed, wailing into my pillows so she wouldn't hear. Suddenly the drama swirling in my head stopped, and I had an epiphany.

I picked up my piano phone and called my mom.

"I want to come home. Forever. I can't live here anymore."

She didn't ask me any questions. She just said okay.

I immediately stopped crying. I was going to show Pam and my dad they had gone too far. I packed up my stuff and wrote my dad a long note. I told him what happened with Pam and that I no longer thought it would be a good idea for me to live with him and *his* family. I felt so empowered that I imagined that by tomorrow, for sure, I'd be getting a call from both Pam and him begging me to come back.

But nothing happened. I barely spoke to my dad or Pam for the next ten years, visiting only on holidays until they got divorced.

I can see now that it wasn't either of their faults. The house was just too small for two teenagers, two babies, and two newlyweds. With Sean and me taking up space, Walter had to sleep in the living room. Being a new mother of two toddlers, a cancer survivor, and a stepmother to two teenagers in a crowded house with a husband who isn't always around is a pretty difficult situation. Of course, Pam was going to snap at whoever was in her range when it all got to be too much for her to handle. Anybody would have, and others probably would have reached that place even sooner than she had. I can see all that now with perspective, age, and experience. I so wish I could go back and slip myself a little note that also asked me to give Pam grace and patience. What if I had said in that moment, *I am sorry it feels that way, but I think you are just really tired, let me take care of Walter and you go take a nap, get in a run, do something for yourself?*

Pam needed support. She needed people from her planet, from our planet, from any planet, to be her team. I am not sure she had built that support yet.

Over the next twenty years, Pam's brain cancer came

back two times. My dad and Pam divorced, and she did develop an amazing group of friends through playing tennis and through her church. In her final years, Pam and I got together sporadically for long talks and began mending our relationship. On our last visit, we both knew that she didn't have long to live.

When she answered the door, half her head was shaved. That gorgeous strawberry-blond hair was still half-there, still shining. She looked so much older, but no cancer or age could ever take away her glowing beauty. I remember being so impressed with that. Even her hands still looked perfectly freckled and gorgeous in those last few weeks.

She told me that her greatest fear was leaving her kids behind before they were ready, and I promised her that I would always look after them. And then we cried about it together. I'm extremely grateful that we were able to heal our relationship and become friends before she died, but I really wish we would have had more time.

That's something I have just, as I am writing this, realized. When Pam died, I cried for my sister and brother. I bawled thinking of them without their mom. I lost it watching Pam's sister speak at her funeral. But I never once let myself cry for me. She was my mom, too, and I think I am just now realizing that I never fully mourned her.

Pam was an unbelievable mother, a great wife, a warrior,

and a solid woman who went through more than most of us can imagine.

Rest in peace, Pam. Thank you for teaching me how to be a mama bear, to cherish life and never take any of it for granted all while making the most kick-ass cranberry muffins with white sauce every Christmas. I really miss my real-life Alien Barbie and can't wait until we can both share the same planet again.

CHAPTER FIVE
LABELS

When someone is on the news, you know that title bar that pops up at the bottom of the screen? We call them *chyrons* (pronounced k-eye-rons) or *lower thirds* in the broadcasting business. They are usually brightly colored graphic bars with bold white text that help identify the person on-screen with their full name, then below that, a quick description or their official title. It's a very useful device in television when you are trying to gather information quickly as you watch a story, but this type of labeling doesn't work well in real life. Each of us is so complex and capable of so much more than one or two titles that can fit on a graphic.

Unfortunately I think many of us get these lifelong chyrons early and can't stop them from popping up when we go out in the world, even if they no longer or never did apply.

While doing a training for diversity and inclusion at work, they gave us a very helpful graph that shows how our identity is built in rings. Think of the center of the target as personality, then the rings around that include race, ethnicity, age, physical ability, gender, and sexual orientation. The next ring includes income, marital status, appearance, recreational habits, educational background, work experience, and religion.

Often, our labels get put on these outermost rings that make up our identity. People assume things about us based on superficial parts of our identity and don't always get to know what's inside those rings.

When we meet someone as an adult, after a bit of small talk about the weather, the most common question is, "What do you do?"

My friend Paula Faris wrote a whole book about this phenomenon and how strange it is that especially in America, our identity is so closely tied to *what* we do, not *who* we are or *what* we are interested in. On the TV chyrons, most of the time it just shows the person's name and title, something like this: MIKE SMITH, PHD, PROFESSOR OF SOCIOLOGY, UNIVERSITY OF MICHIGAN.

Again, important and relevant for a news story, but I have no idea who Mike Smith is.

When I was a kid, I often felt labeled and also labeled myself. My first chyron would have said:

GINGER ZUIDGEEST, GOOD STUDENT.

That one dates to third grade. I was attending Ada

Elementary in the Forest Hills School District of Grand Rapids, Michigan. My parents had just divorced, but in that transitional time my mom moved us from that dream home at Foxfire to a much more modest home in an older subdivision called Ada Croft. After the divorce, I think my little-kid mind was ultra focused on being a good girl, doing everything right, and just avoiding rocking the already tumultuous boat that was my family. So I decided to control my grades. That was something I could do. I loved reading and committed to reading—a lot. Especially when there was extra incentive like we had in third grade. I don't recall the exact deal, but it was something like, for every ten books you read, you got an Eager Reader Badge. Those badges went on a sash and whoever read the most books by the end of the year won a pizza party for their class. Overachiever here, my sash was loaded with badges, and yep, I won the pizza party.

I enjoyed school, so this wasn't a terrible label to have at that time in my life. But it did limit me. If I was a good student, could I also be athletic? Interested in art? Music? Acting? How many words could I fit on that chyron of life?

I was interested in all of these things, but I didn't pursue much outside my studies. I didn't want to ask either parent for more of their time or money or anything that could possibly upset the fragile situation at home, so I studied and read. And proudly kept my lower third, only improving it to GINGER

ZUIDGEEST, GREAT STUDENT. All A's, stellar attendance—my goal of educational perfection only grew stronger.

My brother would get a very different label: SEAN ZUIDGEEST, CREATIVE. This implied that school "wasn't his thing." I always tell the story of my mom saying, "Sean is talented and Ginger is . . . technical." She was mostly referring to music (piano specifically). And she was right. I played piano for ten years starting when I was five. I played well but only because I was so committed, not because I felt it in my bones.

Sean, on the other hand, picked it up immediately, played by ear, and sang like a bird. Though my mom was right, the technical label really wasn't helpful and certainly didn't encourage me to find my creative side. Now, I don't think we should lie to our kids. If they aren't good singers, we shouldn't say they are. Otherwise you end up with an embarrassing early episode of *American Idol* on your hands. Either way, as a parent now, I'm super cognizant of fighting the inherent want to label or identify my children.

During my third-grade year, my dad had moved back to the town he grew up in and it was in a different school district called Northview. When Sean and I stayed with him, he would drive us back and forth to our school. When the school year ended, my mom announced that we would make a move to a new house in the Northview School District "to make it easier on everyone."

My little soul was rocked. It was one thing to have my family fall apart. Now I had to let go of my friends and my perfect attendance record. How would that affect the lower third that I had worked so hard to achieve? There were many questions. I was so dramatic about the move, telling my mom my life would never be the same, that she was ruining everything. All of that from a nine-year-old. She assured me my new school would be even more fun than the current one, and I would love walking to school since our house was right behind it. My dad's house was within a mile of our new one.

That summer was the most tumultuous time in my early childhood. Thinking back on it, I know my poor mom was dealing with an awful lot. Right after my parents divorced, my mom dated our dentist, who my dad let us call Dickhead. Dickhead wined and dined my mom, then left her days before their planned wedding. She was alone again and moving to be closer to her ex-husband. She was working long hours and there were many times when she would come home, drained from overnight shifts at the hospital, and she would blow up.

Our new house in Northview had a loft upstairs with two bedrooms and a TV room where my brother and I spent most of our time. The kitchen was downstairs right off the garage. It was the first room you entered when you came in.

Back then, there was not much that could agitate my mother more than a dirty/messy countertop. To this day, when I'm with my mom and she seems uneasy, my Pavlovian response kicks in and I start clearing all objects from all countertops, then get cleaning products and furiously start scrubbing so there is not a spot or distraction to the eye. A dirty countertop is still my mom's biggest trigger.

One rough day in particular, I remember Sean and I were watching *ALF* while waiting for my mom to get home. I could feel my mom's mood before she even entered the house. I was always an absorber. Far too reactive to other people's feelings. I heard the garage door open, and I could forecast her current disposition by how quickly she pulled into the garage. On this day it was fast. Almost so fast you wondered how she stopped before driving through the walls of the house. The slam of the car door was just another bit of proof that something was wrong. Then the nail in the coffin: I heard her sigh just as she burst through the garage door.

And then my heart stopped for a beat. I thought about the kitchen countertop. It was not clear and it was not clean. Far from it.

I looked at my brother, Sean, eyes wide, and I whispered, "Did you put your bowl in the dishwasher?"

His eyes grew wide now . . . and he shook his head side to side.

His head hadn't even shaken back and forth twice when we heard it.

Slam!

That was her bag.

Crash!

That was likely the bowl.

"FUUUUCKKKKKK."

That was my mom.

"I come home to a messy fucking . . . Ginger Renee! Sean Jeffrey! Get down here NOW!"

Crash!

More things were finding their new resting places from the disorganized kitchen counter to the floor, by way of hitting the wall. The might of this five-foot-three-inch Italian dynamo was impressive. She could make any mess much worse with her temper. My brother and I begrudgingly made our way down the carpeted steps. I was dragging my feet, preparing myself for what would inevitably be my fault.

"What have you two been doing all morning?" she asked calmly as soon as we entered the kitchen. My eyes went straight to her long fingernails rapping on the countertop. It was never good when she had this moment of calm.

It was exactly like the eye of a hurricane. We had already heard and could now see the debris from the first lashing winds of Hurricane Dawn. We were in the deceptive calm of the eye now. What was misleading about this seemingly serene moment was that the second eye wall was minutes or maybe seconds away. You never knew. But much like the second passing of the eye wall of a hurricane, it could be just as terrifying and destructive as the original landfall.

This one was. In fact, I think my mom defied physics.

Sean and I both shrugged, and I said, "We were watching TV." The only thing worse than a dirty countertop is a dirty countertop with two people who were wasting their brains watching TV instead of cleaning or being productive. This time we were in the room to see the storm's fury. A vase on the kitchen table took the brunt of the first gust of Dawn, splintering as it careened off the table, and onto the wall before shattering on the floor. My mom then moved into the living room, flipping chairs, pushing on the table, and almost flipping it in a move that would make Teresa Guidice's eyebrow raise. Anything in her path did not stand a chance.

And then it was over. Just like that. Looking at the two rooms that hurricane Dawn had just blown through, I started picking up the pieces. Silently my brother joined me. We stayed quiet until my mom, now weeping, came over to us as she always did to offer an apology.

"I am so sorry. I just had a really sick baby in the unit last night and four deliveries, and it was just so stressful and to come home to a mess, I just couldn't deal."

We didn't reply. We didn't need to. It was the same story every time. And just like the last time and the next time. We happily accepted her apology. But the calamity still resided inside me. I don't know what my brother was able to do with these moments. But for me, they would upset me for days. My stomach would be unsettled, and I would plot every way I could find to prevent this from happening in the future. What I would learn so many years later is that I couldn't prevent it. That these feelings and these overreactions were my mom's issue. They had nothing to do with me, and even if the counter had been clean (which, from then on, I always made sure of), she still would have had blowups. Because she was tired, because she was lonely, felt disrespected and undervalued, and because her life was not going as she had planned. Most importantly, she had a chemical imbalance that no one knew how to treat and she was never taught the emotional tools she needed to deal with life.

My mom asked medical professionals for help, but they had very little to offer. Years later, she would find that a boost in serotonin helped fix her volatile state. That simple solution was not available in the late 1980s and early 1990s, so she, and we, lived with the consequences. I am so proud of my mom for making it through those times as well as she did. She was always supportive, loving, and there for us. She just couldn't control that one part of herself to no fault of her own. She just needed help.

I have always prided myself on "not having my mom in

me." I would never carry the label HURRICANE GINGER. I just don't blow up.

But it's probably because I don't allow myself to feel. I have practiced, my whole life, not allowing my emotions to rise up. I don't express them, and it's worse than suppressing them—I extinguish them before they are even a thing.

I thought I was Dawn-free because of this . . . but lately I have been working with Dr. Wilson to investigate why I am so obsessed with producing. I allowed part of this mannerism I abhorred in my mom to sneak into my life. My mom is not happy unless she is succeeding, producing, creating. She must be in constant motion. There is no sitting or just being still. Back then she did not have the ability to stop and watch a show on television, let alone a movie.

Dr. Wilson said these were her coping mechanisms. Two ways people cope with anxiety and stress: overachieving and creating structure, or seeming structure. Or, obsession and compulsion.

I am much like my mom—so much so that I have had my husband on many occasions tell me it's okay to just sit. And it's like hearing my dad tell my mom the same thing back at Foxfire. I have to resist the urge to get up and organize a drawer, alphabetize the spices, do anything except be idle. Idle is bad. Idle is not my label.

To combat this, I have to focus and be present, constantly, every second. It's as if I am forcing meditation through life.

Now my lower third was:

GINGER ZUIDGEEST, GOOD STUDENT, OVERACHIEVER, OBEDIENT DAUGHTER.

That fall Sean and I started going to East Oakview Elementary, which, as promised, was right down the hill from our house. On mornings when my mom had to leave before we got off to school, I would get Sean and myself ready proudly. I loved the responsibility; my hair soaking wet, as we were always running late, we would slip and slide down the hill in the winter, my wet hair frozen by the time I sat in Mr. Melpholder's class. I would break the sticks of frozen hair as I settled into my most comfortable place: school.

It was there, at school, in the fall of 1990, that I acquired my next label.

"You like math, don't you, Ginger?" That was my teacher, Mr. Melpholder, after grading my first math quiz.

I did like math. I liked that you had to be right or wrong. I liked that I could show my work and see the progress of an equation. Math just made sense. Those first few days at my new school, I went out at recess and tried to find my way as the new girl, but everyone already had their cliques and I started retreating inside. I asked Mr. Melpholder if I could do extra math problems during recess and filled the time that should have been for play and joy with work and my joy: succeeding. He loved the idea. Of course, I was doing it to avoid the embarrassment that came with being alone at recess, but my teacher didn't know that. Plus, I had to make sure he knew about the overachiever part of my label.

Mr. Melpholder had also taught my dad in elementary school. That's how old he was. He was strict, but I liked him. And unlike my dad (a young immigrant who couldn't speak English and was never a great student), I was quickly becoming the teacher's pet. From a green plastic box, Mr. Melpholder would pull out extra word problems, and I would effortlessly answer them. The only time I hesitated in giving an answer was when my focus wandered, briefly, as I glanced out the window to watch all the girls in my class jumping rope, learning double Dutch (I still can't do double Dutch to this day because of my indoor choice here). Shaking my head, refocusing, I would return to spouting out answers and bury the feelings of loneliness and not fitting in. My label never included SOCIAL during these years.

Our math sessions extended into a world of stamp and coin collecting—things Mr. Melpholder used as rewards for good behavior and grades. I was drowning in stamps and coins by the end of the year. When I lifted the top of my desk, the stamps, sandwiched in their protective cardboard and plastic, would sometimes spill out. The envelopes I had organized them in were overflowing. It was an embarrassment of nerdy riches.

My label now read—GINGER ZUIDGEEST, GREAT STUDENT, ESPECIALLY MATH, OVERACHIEVER, OBEDIENT DAUGHTER.

Mr. Melpholder told my mom at teacher conferences. My mom called my dad's new girlfriend, Pam, and now everyone knew my label.

My label so far was true and it was positive. That would soon change and take me away from what I am doing right now. Writing.

I loved writing. By sixth grade, my social standing had improved. I had developed a group of girlfriends at Highlands Middle School and started holding hands with the cute boys. By sixth grade I was reading a lot of R. L. Stine books and other horror novels like *I Know What You Did Last Summer.* The gorier the better. Murder and mystery were my jam. I loved the drama of it, and I was constantly moved to put pen to paper. I wrote my first real story that year. It was called "Surprise," about a group of friends on summer break. One by one members of their group were murdered. Near each severed head or hand, there was a sign that read SURPRISE and a clue as to where the next killing would happen. It was a little *Scream Queens*–ish now that I think about it. I wrote with blue, pink, and purple ink. I had the pen with all the colors in one. I loved the feeling of expressing myself and smelling the ink on the page, the paper crinkling as I turned it. No computers back then and my mom's old typewriter seemed far from romantic like it does today.

My teacher was so encouraging; she told me the subject

matter was frightening but to keep developing the characters during the summer break. She believed in me. At least I felt that way, and that support encouraged me to keep writing. I went home that summer dedicated to finishing "Surprise" and honing my writing skills.

But back at home, change was afoot again. After my mom's almost-wedding-that-wasn't to Dickhead, she met my stepdad, Carl. In an interesting story, Dickhead and my mom, while engaged, had taken part in a cycling event to raise money for multiple sclerosis research. I think it was a thirty-mile ride. Whatever the distance, it was long enough that a bus picked the participants up at the finish line and took them back to the starting point. On that bus ride back, Dickhead fell asleep and my mom struck up a conversation with the man sitting next to her. They had a great talk, and she told him all about our cottage and her upcoming nuptials. When the bus arrived at the starting line and parking lot, she and the man parted ways as strangers, as we often do on bus rides or airplanes. Grateful for the good company, with no intention of ever seeing each other again.

Fast-forward a few months after the non-wedding, and my mom went to pick up her award for riding in the race—a pair of Ray-Ban sunglasses. I would have ridden thirty miles for those, too! As she exited her car to go grab those sunnies, the man from the bus saw her in the parking lot and ran up to her.

"Oh my gosh, how was the wedding?! Tell me all about it."

My mom informed him that it had never happened. The man felt bad and asked my mom to go see a movie. There was this new one called *Batman*. That man became my stepdad, Carl.

As my mom and Carl got more serious, they bought a house. Lovely that my mom was finally finding support and love, but this house was in a different school district. And just as my happy life was settling, they rocked it. Again. This time was even more upsetting. I had real friends, great teachers, and I was at the head of my class.

GINGER ZUIDGEEST, GREAT STUDENT, ESPECIALLY MATH, OVERACHIEVER, OBEDIENT DAUGHTER, WRITER.

Now I had to start over—again—in seventh grade.

That fall I began junior high at Rockford Middle School. I was most excited about the creative writing class. Excited until I got my first assignment back and it was the first B I had ever received. In red it said *Needs work*.

Wait! I daydreamed like Ralphie in *A Christmas Story* that I stood up and told my teacher that I deserved an A. I went to talk to her after class. She needed to know I was better than B.

We talked and she essentially said, "This is not an A paper, sorry. Maybe writing just isn't your thing."

And from that point forward, WRITER was taken out of

my label. It was that easy. I let someone else tell me what I couldn't do as easily as I let them tell me what I could.

And then I stopped writing. And I reinforced the label.

GINGER ZUIDGEEST, GREAT STUDENT, ESPECIALLY MATH, OVERACHIEVER, OBEDIENT DAUGHTER, BAD WRITER.

That held until four years ago when I published my first book and was told I wasn't the horrible writer I believed I was. And then that book made it on the *New York Times* Bestseller List. That label was so wrong for so long.

But that's the power of labels. One teacher told me I couldn't write. And I believed it. I stopped writing at home. I stopped journaling. And I think this is when the worst of my anorexia and mental-health challenges settled in. When I realized I couldn't control everything in my label, I started controlling something else: my weight.

CHAPTER SIX
Anorexia

Normally Friday was my favorite day of the week because it was Pizza Day at my elementary school. The pizza was never very hot and the cheese stretched more like a plastic substitute than the real thing, but it was a Michelin delicacy for a kid who didn't know better. I would savor every bite with a full-bodied carton of chocolate milk with my friends, and it was heaven.

My love affair with rectangle pizza ended in fourth grade. It was the first Friday at my new school. Even though they also had Pizza Day, I hadn't made any friends and was sitting alone. I stared at the pizza and tried to avoid eye contact with the other kids, who might be teasing me, or worse, feeling sorry for me. I couldn't eat. Ever since my dad and my aunt had teased me for having a "cute belly" at the water park a few weeks before, I had been self-conscious of my body.

It's hard to say at what point I officially became anorexic, but I think the disease took hold of me on Pizza Friday. I might have heard of Tracey Gold's public battle with anorexia (I loved the TV show *Growing Pains*), but I didn't have any friends who had food issues and it wasn't really on my radar. The one thing I do know for sure is that I didn't ask for it.

The lunch bell finally rang, and the cafeteria started buzzing with kids stacking their trays and heading to their next class. I folded and smashed my pizza into an empty chocolate-milk carton to make it look like I had eaten my lunch and headed to the garbage can. I made eye contact with the lunch lady and smiled as I tossed out my uneaten lunch. Fooled. A rush of adrenaline shot through me, like a bank robber taking off in a getaway car. And then I remembered I was a good girl and this must certainly qualify as bad behavior. But I couldn't stop.

Every day after that, I shoved as much of my lunch as I could into an empty milk carton. Hot dogs, hamburgers, lasagna, it all went in there. No longer afraid of sitting alone in the cafeteria, I looked forward to the privacy I needed to pull off my crime. But skipping meals at home was a lot trickier. I would lie to my parents that there was a birthday party with cupcakes at school, or the teachers had surprised us with pizza, and I was still full. I found after-school activities like band practice, then extra oboe lessons, that would make me so late for dinner I'd be excused from the table early to do my homework. I looked forward to the grumbling noise my stomach made when I was hungry, and to my clothes getting loose. But the biggest prize of all was when people started telling me I looked skinny.

I was no longer poor CUTE BELLY GINGER from a broken home. I was SKINNY GINGER, DISCIPLINED GINGER. I was, almost literally, shedding my skin and reinventing myself. And I had a secret, which gave me the power I'd lost when my parents upended my life.

I had no awareness that I was in the throes of a very dangerous disease with the highest death rate of any psychological illness. Anorexics relentlessly push themselves to do better. Oftentimes it extends beyond food issues—we need straight A's, perfect boyfriends, perfect lives. It's an exhausting roller coaster we have no idea how to get off. Every night I'd review what I'd eaten that day and vow to do better the next day. Six grapes would be five, four almonds would be three. It's also a very isolating disease because it's a secret. I spent hours locked away in my bedroom staring at myself in the mirror, pinching fat that didn't exist. I stopped believing people when they said I was skinny. Body dysmorphia becomes the reason we stop listening to parents or teachers who try to help, because obviously they're stupid and can't see that we're fat.

I think I reached the peak of anorexia when I escalated past being obsessed with my body and started being delusional with food. I was attaching value to the shape of foods. For example, I used to eat a lot of baby carrots because they only had five calories each, until I decided that the fatter carrots were riskier than the thin long ones. I truly started believing that a fatter carrot would make a fatter me. My mom used to ask why I had left behind three or four carrots, emphasizing how healthy carrots were for me, for my eyes, how low in calories they were. She obviously had no idea, I thought. When it came to food and my body, nobody could be trusted. Just recently, I felt a wave of anxiety rush over me because I couldn't find a small spoon for the cereal I wanted to eat. It's not all gone. It will never be.

My mom has always been obsessed with her weight and exercise. She would jump up from the table after dinner, put on a Pointer Sisters album, and dance off her dinner. My dad would tease her about a slight belly paunch, of loosening upper-arm muscles, so I'm sure she was at least in part fueled to please him. I'm not saying I wouldn't have gotten anorexia on my own, but there was some foreshadowing from my parents' food issues for sure.

My dad was a health freak. It was less about food and more about the effect his own father's heart attack had on him when I was only four years old. There were lots of foods we were discouraged from eating: sugar, pasta, rice, pizza—they were all "vacant foods" without nutritional value. Which is pretty true, but to a kid it was confusing. A few years ago, Dad gave me a broccoli-sprout tower (to grow my own sprouts) for Christmas. My dad worships at the altar of the broccoli sprout. His cabinets are full of vitamins, and he recently became a strict vegan (no oils; he even avoids nuts and avocados) after a cardiac exam that exposed some calcification of his arteries despite his intense focus on healthy eating. This gave him reason to dive even further into the healthiest pool available. If anybody can make it past a hundred, it's my dad, but sometimes I worry that his asceticism keeps him from enjoying his life. He has created structure to combat his anxiety, and it is on the obsessive side.

Anorexia was my best solution to the powerlessness I felt after the divorce my parents' fighting, their refusal to talk to each other, making me a middleman, and shuttling me to different schools and houses. Nobody ever asked me what I wanted, so I figured it out myself; I wanted to be in charge of my body. I wanted to be skinny.

By seventh grade, I had grown at least six inches to five-foot-five, but I weighed in soaking wet at just ninety-five pounds. I had amenorrhea and was far behind my friends when my period finally arrived just before I turned fifteen. It also somehow stunted my emotional maturity, making even the subject of boys a little frightening.

My parents must have been at their wits' end watching

their daughter disappear before their eyes. So the summer before seventh grade, they sent me to the Netherlands to visit our extended family and travel along with my oma. Maybe my oma could talk some sense into me, or maybe they just needed a break from me. Fine by me. I couldn't wait to spend eight glorious weeks away from my parents' meddling and left in peace to eat (or not eat) as I pleased.

When I landed in Rotterdam, I was terribly jet-lagged. As soon as we got to my oma's cousins' house, the woman I was to call Tante Rika offered me a snack, but I shrugged her off with a "No thank you, I'm really tired." Nobody got upset about it, and I pranced upstairs to my guest room.

The guest room had a full-length mirror that would be perfect for my evening check-ins after sit-ups. I got into bed and quickly fell asleep until the sting of something sugary in my mouth woke me up. I opened my eyes and saw my tiny second cousin standing over me, shrieking with delight.

"Snope! Snope!" (Dutch for candy.)

This cute little five-year-old was gleefully shoving candy into my mouth, but for me it was a full-blown nightmare. I jumped out of bed and spit out the candy and frightened her so badly she shrieked and ran out of the room. There was no way I was going back to sleep.

I went downstairs and sat at the table where everybody was eating. I'd never noticed how voraciously my oma ate her food, down to licking the crumbs off her plate. I'm sure it was an effect of being a World War II survivor, when food was scarce, but it was hard for me to watch. At least nobody made me eat.

After dinner, I went for a walk to burn off the candy calories, and through the windows of every apartment and brownstone home, all I could see was people eating yogurt and custard. They love yogurt and custard in the Netherlands, and it was always the same brand. By now I'd forgotten what it was like to enjoy food, especially dessert. I furrowed my brow at every window thinking, *Those poor people, they have no idea the poison they are pouring down their throats.*

The rest of the trip was slow, and though nobody both- ered me about what I ate, all day long a constant stream of relatives who didn't speak any English came to visit and I was bored. My oma took me for a drive through the countryside, and we had to stop at every house with the same last name as ours because they might be a distant relative. Which was a lot. I started snapping at my oma, acting out as a typical cranky teenager who was also starving herself on 250 to 500 calories a day and thought she was going to be finally left alone on her vacation.

The one bright spot on my trip was when I went to visit my cousin Mario on her houseboat. Mario spoke English and she loved to watch *My Cousin Vinny* in English on her VHS.

We stayed up late and laughed, and the next morning, Mario presented me with a package that had been sent by my mom. I carefully ripped at the brown paper and I even ate a few of the Frosted Mini-Wheats. You know I had to be feeling comfortable if I consumed 210 calories (without milk, 240 with a half cup of skim milk) without so much as a blink of an eye. But after I finished her imported frosted wheat, I began to cry. I needed to get home.

When I got off the plane, my mom didn't look happy to see me. She looked frightened. I was wearing denim shorts from the Limited that had fit me perfectly when I left for the Netherlands, but were now barely hanging on my bony hips. My cheeks were gaunt and my T-shirt looked like it was on a hanger because I weighed only eighty-five pounds.

She hugged me hard and told me she loved me and missed me but that I was way too skinny (not possible to me, but I was used to it). She was crying when she asked if I had eaten at all the last eight weeks. I tried my best to assure her that I was fine, but she wasn't buying it.

"That's it. We are going to Taco Boy right now and you are going to eat something significant. I don't want to lose my daughter."

I tried to put up a fight, but she had something bigger up her sleeve. A threat.

"If you don't eat a burrito, I am going to take you to Pine Rest."

Pine Rest is the mental-health rehabilitation center in our town. She had my attention.

"Pine Rest?! Are you kidding me? Pine Rest is for crazy people!"

My mom wasn't kidding. She was deadly serious. With her giant beautiful eyes popping (that's what my mom's eyes do when she is very serious about something) out of her head, she told me in excruciating detail how the staff at Pine Rest force-fed girls through tubes in their mouths. I was angry that I was being blackmailed. But I get it now. She was watching her daughter starve to death. As a nurse practitioner, she knew exactly the impact that fear has on a stubborn patient.

I knew I was fighting a losing battle, so we compromised. After much back-and-forth negotiation at Taco Boy, I agreed to eat a cheese quesadilla. My mom didn't order anything, and we sat in a booth while she watched me take every bite. I could feel the fattening cheese attaching itself to my cells as she yammered on about me going into therapy, which I also finally agreed to.

Going to therapy was annoying, but I figured out all the tricks to get through it pretty easily. I stuffed my pockets full of more and more pebbles each week when they weighed me in before my session. I lied aggressively and gave all the "right" answers to my therapist's questions, while I silently plotted out my next meal. I made up food I ate in the journal I was supposed to keep every day, sometimes getting ideas like *spring skillet chicken and potatoes* from my mom's *Good Housekeeping* magazines that were strewn around the house. Lying was no longer something I felt bad about; it was survival. I did feel bad that my parents were wasting all this money on therapy, but hey, that was their choice. I had to make my choices a priority.

I was fifteen, and five years into my disease without any signs of it loosening its grip on me. I had lots of rules about food that created a false but very comforting appearance that I was still in control. For example, I would never eat food with any amount of fat content.

One day my mom was making my brother a peanut-butter-and-jelly sandwich before we were all going skiing for the day. I had a photographic memory when it came to nutrition labels, and when I heard *peanut butter* I saw: *2 tablespoons equals 16 grams of fat and 190 calories.* No thanks. My mom didn't even bother to ask if I wanted one. Therapy had brought us one good thing—a truce. The therapist gave my mom strict instructions not to push me too hard about food. I was far from healthy at this point, but at least I wasn't on the verge of hospitalization anymore. But my stepdad, Carl, who was trained in psychology, did not subscribe to the tiptoeing protocol around Ginger's anorexia.

"You know if you eat that peanut butter, skiing will burn more than the calories of that sandwich?"

"Uh, no, Carl I did not know that."

Even with my strict sit-up regimen, it had never occurred
to me that an upgraded level of activity like skiing would allow
for something as forbidden as peanut butter. Carl sensed an
opening and went for it.

"And it's a good fat."

Good. Fat. Not exactly two words I would have strung
together. It was worth considering. Carl was a smart guy who
probably knew what he was talking about. I liked him and he
liked me, and when I scrutinized him for lies, he came up clean.

"Exactly how many calories would I be burning?"

"About four-fifty, I would guess. Maybe more."

Four hundred and fifty. For an anorexic that's like a suitcase full of cash. I ran the math in my head—twenty bags of
carrots or nine apples, or two tablespoons of peanut butter.
On a sandwich. And all I had to do was ski, something that I
loved to do anyway? Count me in, Carl.

This was a huge breakthrough. Extreme exercise was now
my golden ticket, a pass back to the magical land of real food.
And just like food, exercise was something I could control. I
waited for my mom to start making me my sandwich, but she
just stood there holding the knife in her hand, wanting to hug
Carl, but probably afraid to jinx the moment.

I took the jar of peanut butter and carefully measured
out one perfectly level tablespoon and spread it on two pieces
of bread. And then I took a bite. I hadn't had this taste in

my mouth for five years, but it was an old friend I knew and recognized. Thick, smooth, salty, and a little sweet. That one tablespoon brought me so much joy, but I was also buying something I hadn't yet paid for. That day I skied extra hard, and when we got home, I started an "Exercise Journal." My first entry had the date, the 380 calories I ate, and most importantly the 450 calories that the vigorous skiing erased. My debt was paid and I could finally relax.

Because I was eating, the tension in the house receded. Exercise and keeping a journal were time-consuming, but having options besides carrots and apples was fun. I spent more time with my friends, going to sleepovers, and eating a handful of tortilla chips with salsa or a small bowl of air-popped popcorn. I joined my cheerleader friends at the vending machine after practice, splitting a pack of cheese crackers.

Exercise had intensified my anorexic control issues. I kept even more meticulous records of my food and of my exercise. I had even more rituals to keep myself in line and help me resolve to do better the next day. Every morning I did one lap around the kitchen island before taking the Frosted Mini-Wheats cereal from the cupboard. Then I'd do another lap and get the milk. Another lap. A spoon. Lap. Napkin. Lap. Eat a bite. Lap. You get the pattern.

My days were structured and filled with exercise and measured eating. After laps and breakfast, I did squats while brushing my teeth, then two hours of workout shows on ESPN, a 350-calorie lunch followed immediately by a two-mile run. By the time I went off to college, I was so toned, I actually looked much healthier than I was.

During my first semester of college, on top of adjusting to classes and making new friends, I kept up the routine. I loved college, and isolating didn't occur to me anymore. But I couldn't let go of the journal. Finally, sometime during the second semester, I loosened up a bit. My roommate and I would come home late from a party and she loved to order Papa John breadsticks. This was a much higher-risk food than peanut butter or tortilla chips, but maybe because I was drunk enough, one night I gave in and ate one. And then I ate five more. With garlic-butter sauce.

When I woke up the next day and saw the grease stain on my jeans, it might as well have been DNA evidence in a murder trial. I got naked in the mirror, and thank God, nothing had happened to my body. Lesson learned. COLLEGE GINGER was not to be trusted. I worked out all day and refused to write down the breadsticks from the night before.

But it happened again. And again. I was so skinny that it didn't seem to matter, plus my priorities had finally shifted. I wanted a social life. I wanted to be normal. I had my first macaroni and cheese, my first waffle, and my first full cookie in more than a decade, most of them after drinking alcohol.

The summer after my freshman year, I had my first internship in college at WBMA in Birmingham, Alabama. The chief meteorologist, James Spann, was brilliant and became my first mentor. At the end of the summer, James took his three interns to a famous local barbecue restaurant called Dreamland. I looked at the menu and had to ask the waitress what ribs were. James encouraged me to order them, and I ate the entire plate with a side of Wonder Bread. It was like a prisoner who walks out the gates of prison. You were free before you went in, but you've never appreciated it like you do now.

I'd been in prison for ten years, but it's still not entirely clear to me how I got my life back. I wish I could say it was by facing the issues of my childhood in therapy, but it wasn't. Certainly it was some unintentional combination of being happy and busy and the self-medicating power of alcohol. But I also found men in college and that became a new control issue for me. I'll get into how that all went down a little later.

As an adult, I've done a lot of work in therapy on the eating issues as well as on what caused them, but I still spend a lot of time thinking about food. Here's the difference, the healing comes in that moment I realize I can have a thought, but that it's just a thought. I see it and I let it go.

Anorexia, like most psychological issues, is something that can be managed but never fully repaired. Especially with the act of eating, which we have to do every day. I've heard alcohol and drugs compared to a tiger you lock in a cage, while anorexia is a tiger you have to walk around with on a leash all day. Mine had been a *Tiger King* tiger cub at first, used by me to sell the story and get the job done, but I would say now that my anorexia is more like a seemingly well-cared-for Carole Baskin tiger.

But every day I have a choice to be honest about how I'm feeling and to take care of myself. Staying connected with friends and family helps me get out of my head and allows me to see that it's okay to be vulnerable. When I finally admitted that control is not possible, a lot of energy was freed up to enjoy my life.

Change can trigger my control issues. Since I wrote my last book two years ago, there've been a lot of changes in my life. I had another baby, we moved to the suburbs, and there was a global pandemic.

So when I feel the anxiety or fear bubbling up, I bring it up in therapy and focus on what in my life feels out of control. Dr. Wilson has taught me that control is just a coping mechanism. As soon as I look at it this way, it loses some of its power. Meditating every morning is a tool that helps me get ahead of anxiety. I write what I am grateful for on my shower door, and then on the shower wall I write a goal for the day. These practices may seem simple, but they keep me from being overcome by the disease that has ruled so much of my life for the past twenty-seven years.

My anorexia was rooted in control but just as much in

shame. I was ashamed because I blamed myself for my parents' unhappy marriage; I was ashamed to be me.

Every sixty-four minutes somebody dies from anorexia. One out of five anorexics dies by suicide. I'm lucky not to be one of those horrible statistics, so I feel a responsibility to share my story.

Honesty and transparency are part of my recovery. They help my self-esteem and keep my commitment to self-care. And now I eat all the baby carrots no matter their size. I'd say the wider ones even taste a little sweeter these days.

CHAPTER SEVEN
CAMP HUG-A-LOT

The summer of 1995 was one of the most peaceful and happy summers of my childhood. When I close my eyes, I can smell the Sun In, the coconut Banana Boat oil, and the vanilla car freshener that I bought a year and a half in advance of getting my license because I wanted to be ready. Most of the summer was spent at cheerleading practice, cheer camp, soccer camp, and at the houses of my best friends, Alysha and Liz. It was the summer that solidified the three of us as inseparable, and I'm proud to say that we still are today. We were thrilled yet terrified about starting high school, but we were even more occupied by our growing curiosity when it came to boys.

The three of us spent dozens of nights sleeping over at Alysha's house on Lake Bella Vista in Rockford, Michigan—a yellow two-story that was one of the most welcoming and comforting places I had ever been. When you walked into the home, the living room was on the right and a sharp left took you to a wooden door that led you to a finished basement. The basement, where Alysha had her bedroom, was where our clothes-swapping, hair-braiding, girl-talk world flourished.

I'll never forget the decor. It was marine themed. Not just boats and a giant blue anchor, but nets and weathered wood accents everywhere you looked. There was a painting of a fictional captain. While I was writing this, I was convinced that the previous owners had been seafaring folks and Alysha's parents just figured it looked nice, and they lived on a lake so they just embraced it. But when I checked with Alysha to corroborate this memory, I was struck by her humorous response:

"Oh, no, those were my mom's choices. She still decorates like that. The captain hangs in their home in Florida now."

She also reminded me that there was an actual crab trap. We had a really good laugh.

Despite the rough seas of interior design, I would say that basement helped me set sail toward adulthood.

One day, Alysha got very serious after my mom dropped me off for a regular sleepover. She led me through the basement's sliding doors and down the deck stairs, portside (okay, Mrs. Persons [Alysha's mom], I swear I will stop now), to the edge of the lake. I followed her svelte figure and gorgeous shining, long brunette hair down each of the weathered steps. She was dressed impeccably, even though it was a normal

Friday afternoon. Alysha was that always-put-together friend (she eventually won best dressed in high school) in more ways than just her appearance.

If she was the old soul, I was the new soul with so much to learn. She was the friend I yearned to have, the Regina George without all the nastiness. (*Mean Girls* reference. If you haven't seen it, I am sorry. Not sorry I referenced something you don't know, but sorry *for* you, because you are missing an integral part of film history.)

I had no idea what she wanted to talk about, but obviously it was of the utmost importance. Alysha held my hands in hers; her dainty, thin fingers and tiny wrists looked so small compared to my meaty Dutch phalanges.

I looked up from our hand dichotomy just in time for her to look through me with those glittering eyes and she said, "Ginger, you aren't a good hugger."

I just stared at her. My wide fingers let her doll-like hands drop. I mean, I knew I wasn't a great hugger, but so what?

I came from a family of non-huggers. We did it, but only when it was required, and not very well. In my mind, hugs were meaningless and not at all interesting. You go in, wrap your arms around whoever, but not too tight, tap the other person's back a few times, and go on with your day. Recently the kids at school had been hugging each other more than what I thought was normal, but it didn't bother me. So why did it bother Alysha so much that I was bad at it?

"Kissing and hugging go together. So if we're going to get you your first kiss, you're gonna need work on your hug. And you should just be better at hugging in general. For life."

Alysha was often right, and this time she was dead-on. I was fifteen and way behind my girlfriends when it came to boys. My sexual résumé so far included holding hands a few times in the hallway at school, and once a "boyfriend" put his arm around me at a basketball game. Not the depth of experience one might have seen in other almost-ninth-graders. Alysha had progressed from hugging well into kissing, so she was the perfect instructor.

And that's how the hugging workshop I call Camp Hug-A-Lot began.

Alysha came from a tight-knit family that did a lot of hugging. Her dad is a big teddy bear and her mom is a gentle, loving woman. It made sense that Alysha was so confident about being physical with boys; she was fearless, a loyal friend, and positively perfect in my eyes. If she said hugging was important, I believed her.

According to Alysha, the first step to a good hug was a neutral one arm over and one arm under. Then you wait for the boy to move in closer until your bodies touch. As Alysha demonstrated, I could feel her warm breath on my ear and neck as she hung her head over my shoulder and explained it all step-by-step. Even though she was one of my best friends,

111

and I had yearned for closeness in our friendship, I was extremely uncomfortable, and I kept telling myself over and over to resist the urge to pull away from her. I knew she was here to help me. So I stayed put.

Each time we practiced, I kept daydreaming about escape plans. One had me jumping in the lake behind her house and swimming away as fast as I could. As I winced and she held on I wondered, *Why can't I just be one of those people who likes this and feels at peace with it?* Or, *Why can't I simply be a non-hugger and everyone else can deal with it?* Innately some people just require less touch. I consider myself a likable person and I'm very friendly, but even after Camp Hug-A-Lot concluded and my skill was honed, it was and still isn't easy for me to hold a hug or to enjoy it. Most of my life I've heard myself described as "detached" and "cold" when it comes to physical touch and emotional connections.

According to my mom, when I was a baby, as soon as I was done nursing, I would push her away. When my brother, on the other hand, was finished, he would cuddle up into my mom's shoulder and fall asleep.

When my husband and I recently bought our home, he put his arms around me as we looked over our new backyard. The hugging thing has always been a joke between us, so he laughed and said, "You are so uncomfortable right now, aren't you?" Then I laughed because, of course, I was.

To some degree, I was probably just born this way. It's my nature. But I can't dismiss the nurture factor, because as I said earlier, nobody in my family is a great or frequent hugger. And many years after Camp Hug-A-Lot, I would learn that my aversion was a representation of my inability to express my emotions. Today I know that hugs can actually lead to better mental and physical health.

My dad isn't one to initiate a hug, and his hugs are on the rough side. He is incredibly muscular and, for lack of a better word, stiff. When my brother and I were little, he did give us gigantic bear hugs before bed because it was our ritual. It was fun but never mushy. My mom's hugs have always been good, but they are given on a need-to-hug basis, like if she hasn't seen you for a year. My mom was always distracted, not detached like me. She enjoyed hugging and never shied away from it; she just forgot sometimes.

My husband's family is the complete opposite of mine. He grew up hugging his parents every morning, and even now it seems like all they want to do is hug. They've even helped me get a little more used to hugging. My mother-in-law, Janis, stayed with us for more than a month two summers ago and every day she would come up from the basement where she and my father-in-law stayed, and before heading out to Starbucks she would not only hug everyone in the room, but kiss them, too. It really showed me how different Ben's upbringing was . . . and how unique mine might have been.

I recently texted my brother to make sure my memory of our family's lack of hugging was clear.

Why is it that you and I don't like affection? Did we ever kiss and hug in our family, or am I blocking something out?

My brother responded with this haunting line:

I don't remember hugs and kisses. I remember hellos and good-byes.

For this reason, the subject of wanting affection, or my lack thereof, is a common one in my sessions with Dr. Wilson. Dr. Wilson says it isn't the frequency of the affection you get from your family that counts, but the energy behind it—i.e., one long, authentic hug counts way more than a thousand quick, stiff hugs. Sean and I had neither the warmth nor the frequency.

As for energy, my mom has an abundance of it, but it can be overwhelming in its intensity. Dr. Wilson calls it "flooding energy." Her emotions were explosive and unpredictable. They erupted like a flash flood rushing down a mountainside, washing us away in the current. As a defense mechanism, I had to build a dam to protect myself from her flood. So even if she had a genuinely warm hug, I might have not been able to receive all of it.

My dad shut off his energy. I had the feeling that he thought too much affection was corny, so I continually "required" less. My reaction was to pretend not to care. My dad exhibits a different sort of unpredictability, a much quieter one that is more difficult to forecast because he doesn't give off loud signals like my mom. He also has a unique way of communicating. My sister and I joke that we are fluent in a language called Bob-Speak. When I wrote him with the great news that I got a new job in New York City, his response was, "New York is a dirty city." Translated from Bob-Speak, that means "I'm proud of you."

Dr. Wilson explained that a hug is one of the most vulnerable things we can experience. A hug shows the hug-ee you need them, that they are being allowed into your emotional space. In some instances, a hug can reveal that you've hit the peak of your emotional arousal. That's one of the reasons a hug can help you feel better. Much like tears, when our bodies reach a tipping point of emotional arousal, we need to break the nervous-system tension, and a hug can do the trick!

In a recent therapy session, I had a revelation: I never let myself *feel* enough to get that aroused. So I never needed a hug to fix it.

It's likely my dad has never been comfortable with the vulnerability of a hug and neither have I. I don't want anybody to think I need their hug—or frankly that I need them for anything at all. I don't cry at things I am supposed to cry at (you will learn more about that in the following chapters).

I don't cry when I am happy, sad, or excited. It was never safe for me, so I conditioned myself to suppress any display of emotional vulnerability.

It's a self-defense and self-efficiency mechanism that protects me from people who might hurt me. As I make better choices about the people I allow into my life and create stronger boundaries, I hope hugging will keep getting easier. When I think back to who I have hugged effortlessly, the list is short and includes mostly children. They don't challenge my emotions. They are safe, forgiving, and we know they need us.

Hugging my children is easy for me. Kids thrive on the reassurance of a hug, and it makes me feel good providing that for them. If you saw me with my kids, you would never know I have a hugging issue. I cherish the closeness I have with my boys, particularly because I know they won't let me hug them forever. I want them to feel the security I never had as a kid. Hugging them has helped me realize that it's okay to depend on the right people. We just have to make a decision to let go and let them in.

But it's not just about hugging them. I need to work on hugging other people *for* them. I need to combat my history and rid my brain of the default setting: hugs are meaningless and a waste of time. I need to see and feel the difference. I need to work to allow myself to feel and be vulnerable enough to say, "I need help managing this emotion." I've heard many people say, "I could really use a hug." Now that I am in a safe environment, when I set goals for the day (after my gratitude exercise), I write *Hug more.* Hug my children more, of course, but hug Ben more. Even when I don't want to. Like sit-ups, hugging has benefits. And eventually I hope to say, "I could really use a hug" and mean it!

Working in news for the past two decades, I have seen countless stories about how hugs are scientifically related to being healthier. Lowering blood pressure, improving immune systems, and overall lowering stress on the heart. Most importantly to me: A parent who gives lots of hugs to their child sets them up for a healthier future both mentally and physically.

In my first book, I detailed a therapy tool of mine called "the fence," which allowed me to create boundaries and determine who I wanted to get close to. The fence gave me back my power. It took some time getting used to the fence, and initially I used it as another wall to keep people out. I give my husband a lot of credit for hanging in there. Once I let him in, it was such a positive experience that it felt okay to try it again.

Now I am committed to giving Ben the vulnerability he deserves. His love language is touch and I am working so hard to become fluent for him. He sees the work and appreciates it.

If you think of yourself as a non-hugger, or maybe it's just not your favorite thing, I hope my story inspires you to ask why. Dive in and ask yourself if it is something you would like to address, and I promise you the answers will come.

Back at Camp Hug-A-Lot, we didn't dig that deeply. Hugging was a social skill I needed to learn with one goal in mind. Alysha had a three-step program that was easy and simple enough that even I could follow.

First there was the approach, then the follow-through, and finally the smooth pull-back. Liz and I had to practice on each other until Alysha was satisfied that I was ready to take my skills out into the real world. To her credit, I did get my first kiss just two months later.

CHAPTER EIGHT
SEX

The year was 1991 and I was ten years old. My mom was driving and the radio was blaring Salt-N-Pepa's racy-for-a-ten-year-old hit song "Let's Talk about Sex." I was really getting into the music, singing loud and bobbing my head, when I realized *what* I was singing. In front of my mom. Maybe because I stopped, she noticed, too.

"Ging . . . you want to talk about sex?"

"Ugh! No, I do not and stop smiling, Mom!" My mom was obviously loving every minute. She had a familiar twinkle in her eye that meant this was a twofer: a funny story she could tell her friends and a teachable moment as a mom.

Besides, she knew I knew about sex already. She'd given me the full "anatomy discussion" when I was just six years old. My best friend at the time, Alexandra, and I were riding in the backseat of my mom's maroon station wagon after piano lessons when Alexandra told me she knew where babies came

from. She was very familiar with the female and male anato-
mies and knew how men and women used the parts to make
a baby. Alexandra's green bow, attached to her long, dark
braid, swayed as she peppered her conversation with words
I'd never heard before like *ovary* and *ejaculation*. All of that
from a six-year-old (her parents were doctors). The minute we
walked through the front door after Alexandra's primer, my
mom gave me a clinical version of the baby-making process
using words I'd also never heard of before, like *egg fertilization*,
sperm, and *cervix*.

Now that I was in fifth grade, some of my friends were getting their periods and they acted as if they were on the cusp of
womanhood and sex. Not me. I wouldn't get my period until
I was almost fifteen, so maybe they were right, and interest
in boys was connected to a woman's cycle. I'd recently heard
of kids at school talking about orgasms and orgies. I played it
cool, but I had no idea what they were talking about until I
looked the words up in the big brown dictionary on my desk
at home. That dictionary was the closest thing we had to
Google in those days, but thankfully, it had a much more dis-
creet search history. That run from the bus into my bedroom
where the dictionary was kept was always a fast one, with me
repeating the words I didn't dare write down, but needed to
remember so I could look them up as soon as I rolled open the
deep cherrywood of that old-school banker's desk.

I had, however, recently crossed the kissing threshold with a boy I had had a crush on for a while; his name was Kevin Hanrahan. Isn't that funny how we always remember the first and last name of our first crushes? As if he could never be called just Kevin. Always Kevin Hanrahan. That fateful night at a roller-skating party, Kevin Hanrahan (okay, I will go with Kevin from here on out) kept glancing at me. But then he would go out and show off his skating skills, smooth and rhythmic, as his perfectly spiked brown hair never moved because it was smothered in Dep hair gel. I knew it was Dep because it smelled like my brother's hair gel, and I had been close enough to Kevin to take a whiff when he stopped by where my friends and I were talking. It was Dep for sure, but it smelled even better because it was on Kevin. The second time he stopped by, that piano intro to the hit Bryan Adams song began. "Everything I Do, I Do It for You" was one of the biggest hits of the year and I knew every word. Rather than sing them out loud like I usually did into my hairbrush while swinging around my bedpost at home, I just smiled quietly, internalizing every word, as if Kevin were singing them straight to me. We skated together and held hands several times, and at the end of the night, he guided me off the rink for a soda. As we took off our skates and changed into our shoes, I prepared myself for the big moment as I looped that last part of my lace on my white Keds, and then the record stopped.

He said, "My mom is here to pick me up, bye!"

The *bye* was said with his cute face already turned toward the exit and away from me.

How did I misread the signals so badly? How did this night end in such an unceremonious way? I was 10 percent relieved because I had been so nervous to finally get my first kiss, but most of me was ready and now I was so disappointed.

Suddenly, like we were in a cheesy but totally romantic Hallmark movie, Kevin turned around, ran back to me, leaned in, and kissed me.

The kiss was super short but very, very sweet. Our lips were closed and it may have been only one millisecond longer than a peck, but either way, I had officially been kissed. I forgot all about my family and my anorexia and anything negative around me. Somebody I wanted to kiss wanted to kiss me. Life was good.

From that first fifth-grade peck to the next time I would have a kiss would be about four years. I switched schools for a second time in my young life and had to start over. Fortunately I found Alysha and Liz pretty quickly at Rockford Middle School and our best-friend group was solidified by the summer before my freshman year.

Right after Camp Hug-A-Lot concluded during the summer after eighth grade, Alysha decided she had to explain the steps that happened after kissing. Alysha was and still is "the mature one" in our group—the most loyal and committed friend anyone could have; any criticism was always fueled by genuine concern for her friends. During this particular sleepover, we retired belowdecks—I mean, to the basement. We would sit and talk for hours on the blue couch. This night, the discussion surrounded Alysha's genuine concerns that we were falling behind on the dating front. Considering I hadn't even french-kissed a boy, I thought she was overestimating the leap I could make next.

Soon after that sleepover, Alysha helped introduce me to Sam Himmelspach. I appreciated that she thought he was a possible candidate for me, but again I thought she was being a little ambitious on my behalf.

Sam was by far the most handsome boy at our school and he was a year older than me. He had huge, brown, soulful eyes, the most beautiful skin, and the sweetest smile. He looked like a twenty-year-old grown-up, and I still felt like a little kid. He ran every room he was in with the most fun-loving, boisterous energy paired with charm and empathy. He was the guy with so much school spirit, he painted his body with a few friends to pump up the crowds at our Friday-night football games. You know, *that* guy.

After a few introductions from Alysha and her boyfriend, and a conversation or two on the phone, Sam asked me to be his girlfriend. That's really how it all happened back then;

the courting process was so much simpler. Sam was not technically my first boyfriend, but he was my first high-school boyfriend. Just two weeks later, when school started, I still couldn't believe that I was walking down the hallway of my school holding hands with Sam Himmelspach.

We held hands at football games, we held hands at each other's house, we held hands at friends' parties—we held hands a lot. But for weeks I delayed the french kiss because I was just too nervous. How could I live up to Sam's kissing standards? I knew I wasn't his first kiss. It became almost a joke when two months later we still hadn't frenched. This kiss got so built up and put off that it almost had to happen at the most John Hughes–worthy setting: the homecoming dance.

As homecoming approached, I knew the kiss was inevitable, and I knew there had to be tongue for it to count. Alysha coached me through it, mostly reminding me that "it's really not a big deal. It will just happen naturally." Even Sam and his friend Steve helped me navigate my nerves by talking about it freely.

We would often all hang out at Steve's house, chatting in the basement or at a bonfire in the backyard. My friends would create the perfect setting for me to feel relaxed, leaving Sam and me alone. We got so close so many times and Sam was so patient.

Sam always emphasized that we could wait until I was

ready. As I write this, it is so quaint to me that he was so patient, but I am almost annoyed with myself back then. We weren't talking about my virginity here, just a kiss, so I was definitely making it more difficult than it had to be. But like most other great men who would come into my life, Sam knew it wasn't about what was easy or should be, but what I needed. He listened, and ultimately, he respected me.

The night of the homecoming dance, I took my time getting dressed after I went to the nicest salon in town, Design 1, where they curled my hair and pinned most of it back, but left those two long tendrils, perfectly coiled and perfectly 90s, to hang from each side of my forehead. Once I had applied more makeup than I normally did (for me that meant a little blush and a touch of eye shadow), I passed the time posing awkwardly for photos that my mom insisted on taking. This was a time well before social media, so my poses were just using whatever was around me and as far as possible from the curated images you might see teenagers take today.

"Grab the phone and pretend you are making a call," my mom instructed. That phone in my mom's bedroom was a rotary with the dial covered in gold plate, an ivory handset, and a cord that could stretch to the next bedroom. I twirled the cord as I glanced up with my blue eyes, which that night had a hint of green because the light was bouncing off the color of my shiny, emerald-green satin dress.

My mom knew nothing of Operation French Kiss that was about to ensue. I heard the doorbell ring and sauntered down the stairs; the emerald-green dress had a halter top, a sweetheart neckline, and a structured bodice; my mom bought it for me at the fancy Hudson's department store. I wore a long costume-jewelry necklace that contained at least forty carats of cubic zirconia gems; it fell into a drop with matching clip-on earrings (I still hadn't had my ears pierced), and I had sprayed a lot of my best Elizabeth Arden Sunflowers perfume across my collarbone. Sam would not be kissing a kid this evening.

My mom and Carl had just finished an addition to their farmhouse. The original home, built in the 1850s, featured dark cherrywood, so they had matched the staircase and the door in the addition. That wide door, half glass on top, dark cherry on the bottom, had an old-school doorbell with a brass finish. It looks like a key, and when you turn it, it sounds like a bicycle horn. Sam was looking down at the unique doorbell trying to figure out how to use it, when he looked up to find me standing on the stairs straight ahead of him.

My heart jumped into my throat, then fell into my stomach. He was so handsome, dressed in a gray suit, his facial hair trimmed, and the smile he gave me through that glass on the door was brighter than I had ever seen. If I didn't lock this guy down tonight with a french kiss, there was something wrong with me, I thought.

I smiled back through my clear braces and opened the door. He leaned in to kiss my cheek and whispered in my ear, "You are so beautiful."

We shared niceties with his parents and my parents and started taking photos together. As he slid the white flower corsage on my wrist, full of mini roses, my nerves started to calm. Sam put his arm through mine and we headed off into the night.

After a nice dinner, we pulled up to the school, which was decorated with streamers and glitter confetti; the theme was Knight in Shining Armor. Sam offered to get us some water, and when he walked away, my nerves returned. The night was a touch awkward with all these high schoolers head-banging and sweaty as we danced to the odd combination of Nirvana and a lot of Ace of Base. Finally Sam pulled me onto the dance floor for the first slow song.

I glanced over to Alysha and she gave me a thumbs-up and a wink. I looked the other way and Steve was doing a pelvic thrust toward Sam but stopped as soon as my eyes met his. And then all the other faces, the teenage chatter that hummed through the air, it all melted away and it was just Sam and me in a school cafeteria with a spotlight on us. Okay, no real spotlight, but it felt like there should have been.

"Glory of Love" by Peter Cetera started playing. Sam gave me a reassuring smile. He took his hands from my waist, the accepted slow-dance position, and moved one to my lower back and another to my face.

He was going for it. I barely had time to react or protest. Right there in front of everybody, he leaned in and we kissed. It happened so quickly, but lasted a whole lot longer than that kiss at the roller-skating rink. The Band-Aid had been ripped off, and Alysha was right, it really wasn't that big of a deal. In fact, I enjoyed it. No wonder people do it all the time!

We kissed a lot more the next few weeks, and I think I fell in love. Okay, lust. I would stare at Sam's photo before bed and even kiss it good night. When our phone calls became less frequent and our hangouts more dotted in the calendar, I could feel the relationship ending.

A few months after that kiss, Sam broke up with me for a girl in his own grade who had giant boobs (I'm sure she had many other positive qualities, but I was fourteen, so our physical differences were all I could see). I barely fit into an A-cup and the breakup devastated me. I listened to sad songs like Mariah Carey's cover of "Open Arms" over and over and over again on my giant boom box CD player and hoped that Sam would call and beg me to come back. Of course that never happened, and of course I got over Sam. Less than a year later, I met my first soul mate: Leo.

Over the next five years, Leo would play a major role in my life all the way through to my sophomore year of college.

I called him my first soul mate because I believe that we can have multiple soul mates throughout our lives, but the first one is special. Leo changed the way I saw the world and myself. We met our sophomore year of high school in an earth science class. I already knew that I loved science and especially weather, but this was the class that started me thinking that I wanted it to be my career. Leo was the cherry on top.

Leo was brilliant and incredibly handsome, with a mega-watt smile, deep dimples, tight curly hair, and a lean sinewy body that was somewhere between a boy and a man. He started flirting with me in our pre-SAT sessions, and I flirted back. By the end of our sophomore year, we were going steady and I was actually in love. Not just lust.

We were best friends who loved each other and there wasn't anybody else whose company I enjoyed more. We were together almost every day. He was the boyfriend who regularly surprised me with romantic gestures, like leaving a dozen red roses in my locker for absolutely no reason.

Take all of that amazingness away and you can get to the real psychology of why Leo and I became so inseparable. When I was fourteen, Bridget was born to my dad and Pam. At fifteen, Adrianna was born to my mom and Carl. At sixteen, Walter was born to my dad and Pam.

My parents had started new families, and while they did

their best to make Sean and me feel included, it was impossible for us to have the attention or love we would have had if they had just remained divorced.

Leo filled a huge void in my life after my parents got busy with their new spouses and new babies. He was a solid, dependable presence. When I looked up in the stands at my soccer games, Leo was there. Cheerleading competitions, Leo was there. My parents came when they could, but it was far from every time.

Leo was. Always. There.

He called me *princess* and cherished me. He set the precedent for how all men should treat women. Like Sam, he listened, asked questions, and had big dreams, not just for himself, but for us together.

We respected each other's ambitions and made a pact not to drink, smoke, or do drugs. We didn't want to take any risks that would derail our dreams. We talked about our future as high-school sweethearts who get married and stay together forever. Because, why not? His parents had done it.

Sometimes I wish I could have fulfilled those promises, but as necessary as that relationship was in high school, it was far too much responsibility for me once I got to college.

Leo went to a university in Michigan and I went off to Valparaiso University. We broke up and got back together several times during the next four years, but it wouldn't be until almost two years after college that it was officially over. Leaving Leo for good was one of the most difficult separations because he played that combination role of first love and parent fill-in.

When the breakup finally did happen, Leo was already successful in his business and I was working at the NBC affiliate in Flint. We had decided to give it one last shot now that we were adults. We went on two dates, and just like it always had, it felt comfortable, safe, and solid.

In my mental-health state at the time, those were not the qualities that I found attractive. I wanted pandemonium and pain. I am so sorry, Leo. I just wasn't healthy and I was not fair to you.

Just after our second last-chance-ever-for-us date, I had a manic moment and decided to pick up and go to California, because I had a bad feeling that Bob Barker was going to die (I was way off, obviously), and I just needed to be in the audience of *The Price Is Right*. While there, I fell in love with a guy named Joe Frost, another audience member (full, weird story in *Natural Disaster*, if you're interested), who happened to also be from Michigan. It turned out to be a bit more than a vacation fling (I dated Joe for six months after that trip), so when I returned I told Leo that we were over, and he knew that I meant it. And he told me he was never coming back.

Leo was one of three men in my life I had a relationship

with besides my husband that wasn't based on sex. He loved me unconditionally, and I thrived. Being a Goody Two-Shoes wasn't something to be embarrassed about. It meant I was smart and my dreams mattered. SEXY was not a label I felt I needed to have when I was with Leo.

When I got to college, it was.

CHAPTER NINE
SEXY MAMA

"Walk like you do when you are being sexy for your husband."

My *Dancing with the Stars* partner, Val Chmerkovskiy, was serious, but I had to laugh at his instruction.

We'd been partners for about three weeks, and he was giving it his best to ease me into the samba, a Latin dance that we had been assigned for the second week of competition. Our first dance was the jive and it had come easily to me; the staccato, hyper, happy-go-lucky energy suited my personality, or at least the mask of the personality I had perfected for so long. Afterward, Val compared my smile in that dance to a golden retriever sticking his head out of a moving car. I didn't disagree or mind that comparison at all because I was truly feeling the joy of dancing. But golden retrievers don't have to be sexy. Samba dancers do.

By this point, Val had worked with nearly a dozen partners, each of whom had different skill levels. I was the first brand-new mom he had ever trained. I would have loved to blame my inability to "walk sexy" on the fact that I just had a C-section or that I'd been married for a few years, but the truth was my "sexy side" had been muted for a long time.

My husband, Ben, and I are goofy together, so that sets a precedent, but I hadn't been feeling sexy for a few years. And it wasn't just with Ben. I felt like I'd lost my mojo, and I had no idea how Stella was going to get her groove back.

Before my marriage I had dated a lot. One Christmas my mom thought it was funny to get a garland of gingerbread men and write the name of every boyfriend I had ever had on the gingerbread. Ginger's (bread) men . . . get it? Not embarrassing at all, Mom. She also said to Ben soon after we were engaged, "Thank goodness you didn't meet Ginger during her promiscuous days."

That's being a bit generous, Mom. The truth was my promiscuous days were actually years. Starting in my twenties, men were my obsession or even drug of choice. They gave me a high like nothing in the world. And it wasn't about sex; the high was the attention I got from them and the void they filled that briefly buoyed my self-worth. Of course, like any drug, it didn't take long for the high to wear off, and soon I'd go on the hunt for another guy. Even when I was still in a relationship. I regret that I behaved this way and regret the pain I may have caused, but it was a compulsion to keep getting that rush of attention that comes at the beginning of a relationship. I take responsibility for my narcissism and for putting my feelings first. But now that I have dissected it all a bit more, I actually don't think I was putting my feelings first. I don't think I was having feelings.

My sexual awakening happened my freshman year at Valparaiso thanks to my OA (orientation assistant), Luke. Luke was a senior, and he had beautiful dark skin, a bright white smile, and a twinkle in his eyes that said, "Let's make some trouble." Luke initiated the flirting almost as soon as we met. We had an immediate, powerful chemistry together that was like an unstoppable bullet train. I was still with Leo, with whom my chemistry had mellowed to more of a solid and consistent commuter train. Leo nurtured and protected me, but I also felt like a little girl with him. Luke saw me as a woman, and I wanted nothing more than to see that in myself.

The night before classes started, Luke invited me and my roommate to a party at his apartment. I took a lot of time putting my late-grunge-era, 1999 outfit together (flannel shirt tied at the waist, huge jeans), and I even put on makeup, which was not a regular thing for me at the time. I almost asked to borrow the dark lip liner I had seen on one of the girls across the hall, thinking that I could leave the inside part of my lip natural colored like they did in the magazines, but I opted for a more natural swipe of the only lip gloss I owned, so I wouldn't look like I was trying too hard.

The second Kirsten and I walked into the party, I saw Luke across the crowded room.

"Hey, gorgeous!"

I turned and looked behind me to see who he was talking to. Me? My cheeks flushed and then my neck, and then it rushed down my body all the way to my toes. When Luke grabbed my hand and swept his fingers across my collarbone, his sexual energy transferred to me like an electric shock. I'm sure he felt it, too.

He asked if I wanted a drink, and even though I'd never had a drink in my life (I know—ears still were not pierced and I had not had a drink thanks to the promise Leo and I had made to each other), I said, "Sure."

"Beer? Wine?"

"Wine," I blurted out.

He returned with a Solo cup filled with a syrupy-looking red liquid that smelled like strawberries and medicine. I lifted it to my mouth to take a sip and ANOREXIC GINGER shouted at me that there were 250 calories in this cup. But SEXY GINGER, who had been born about five minutes ago, shouted right back, *Shut up and have some fun!*

The wine was sweet and moved like a warm river down my body, and the nervousness disappeared like magic. Luke and I began to dance to "You Make Me Wanna" by Usher, and when he held me tight, I didn't feel cute or pretty—I felt hot. I had never considered myself to have any dancing skills, but it was easy to follow Luke's lead. Pretty soon we were moving our hips together like Jennifer Grey and Patrick Swayze in the Catskills. It's a great reminder to me even now that sexy really doesn't have anything to do with the act of sex. It's an attitude, an energy, and I loved it.

And then I thought of Leo. I stopped dancing and pushed Luke away, saying I had to use the bathroom. I went looking for Kirsten because I needed to leave. I didn't want to cheat on Leo. I knew that was wrong and I had too much respect for him to cheat. If I stayed here with Luke for one more minute, none of that would matter. Kirsten was at the back of the party smoking with a guy I'd never seen before. I tugged on her shirt and told her we had to go.

Kirsten didn't get it and I was too embarrassed to explain. Besides, I didn't really want to leave! SEXY GINGER was in the house and she was very persuasive. *You're a college woman now! It's time to stop acting like a little girl and do what makes you feel good!* SEXY GINGER was loud.

Luke found me and asked if he had moved too fast. I wanted to grab him, push him against the wall, and kiss him, but my better self prevailed. I told him about Leo and apologized for flirting and leading him on. And then he gave me that twinkle in his eyes and smile.

"Well, if he ever messes up, get your sexy ass straight to me."

Luke didn't just dance to Usher, he was like Usher come to life. What kind of college student talks like that?

Nothing happened between us that night, but it was a pivotal moment for me. I saw what he saw, a sexy young woman, and with that newfound label and confidence, I was off to the races.

I walked into my first class of that first semester of college full of the kind of mojo that deserves a slow-motion entrance with a soundtrack. Never mind that it was calculus, my pheromones were on. A very cute guy I'd never met before waved at me to sit next to him and introduced himself as Michael. He was handsome and had a remarkable magnetic personality. We immediately had chemistry. Chemistry, in calculus class.

Michael made it clear that he wanted to be more than friends pretty quickly, but I was up-front about being involved with Leo this time. I didn't expect it, but my honesty seemed to make him want me more. I enjoyed the power and confidence of our dynamic, and everything I was learning about being a "sexy" woman.

Leo and I still talked almost every night. I'd sit on my bed in the dorm room twirling the landline phone cord, being nice but a little distant and bored. Sometimes I'd lose patience with Leo over some tiny, meaningless thing and I'd feel bad. I was frustrated that I couldn't break up with him. I mean, I could have, of course, but that growing part of me that wanted to end it was thwarted by the constant reminder that if Leo was gone, I would have to find someone who could fill that parent role I had come to expect embedded in a boyfriend.

The prospect of being with Michael continued to erode the attraction to the stability Leo offered. Sometime in early spring of our second semester, Michael snuck into my dorm room early in the morning and splashed a mimosa in my face. I know, not exactly the stuff of a rom-com but I liked it.

"Get up. Let me see you."

I got out of bed and stood next to him. He made me feel like Gisele Bündchen in a T-shirt and boxer shorts.

"You are a fucking knockout."

At this moment, imagine me turning to the camera and breaking the fourth wall like John Cusack in *High Fidelity* when he says about Catherine Zeta-Jones, "She actually talks like that." Mike actually talked like that. His fearlessness made him irresistible. He playfully slapped my ass and pulled me in for a kiss on the cheek, always pushing the appropriate line, pulling me close enough that we might as well have been having sex but were fully clothed and being "good."

"Get dressed. We're going to the Cubs game."

One of Michael's friends had parents with front-row seats at Wrigley Field. By 10 a.m., five of us were on our way to Chicago, and four of us were already drunk when we got there. Our hands were all over each other throughout the game. When the Cubs got a run, he picked me up; when the pitcher struck a player out, I grabbed his face. Even when a player hit a foul ball, it was a justification to touch each other.

I excused myself to get a round of beer at the concession stand. I didn't have an ID, but somehow that didn't matter. Heading back, I was looking at the stands to find my friends when Mike turned around and caught my eye. He had started crawling over people to come help me with the huge trayful of beer, when suddenly the crowd erupted. Neither of us had been watching the game, but a Cub hit a home run. The stadium was roaring, and I hoisted the tray triumphantly above my head in celebration as Mike finally broke free and sprinted up the steps to lift me. I wrapped my arms around him and then my legs, dropping the beers and all pretense of staying faithful to my boyfriend. It was a scene rivaling *The Bachelor* meet-ups. We not only kissed but made out until an usher asked us to move. The irritated popcorn and hot-dog vendor actually bumped us out of his way. We spent the rest of that game basking in the flood of relief that eight months of pent-up teasing will get you.

As soon as I got back to my dorm room, the buzz of happiness and euphoria I had felt with Mike came crashing down on me. I called Leo and finally broke up with him, mentioning Michael and apologizing, but knowing I would need that to solidify the breakup. It felt good to be honest and to have that scapegoat because any other time I had brought up spending time apart, Leo had been able to talk me out of it.

Michael and I started dating, and my life immediately got so much easier. Sure, it helped that I was in lust, but I think it was the freedom I gave myself to be a sexy, confident woman. I got straight A's in all my classes without working nearly as hard as I had to in high school, and Michael asked me to come home with him for spring break. I was pretty confident this meant he wanted to take our relationship to the next level. Obviously we were on our road to getting married. (If you read my first book, you know how quickly I jumped to that place). I had the emotional maturity of an eighth grader and I expected every man to want forever with me like Leo had.

Michael's family was warm and welcoming, the kind of family I could see myself becoming a part of. Again, slow down, Ginger. We ate dinner together every night on that trip, went to his brother's baseball games, and celebrated Mike's twentieth birthday.

Back on campus, it felt like our friends were relieved that we had finally crossed into a romantic relationship. It was all just way too good to actually be true. One night, as we studied for a Calc 2 exam, a friend of Mike's accidentally revealed the big secret Mike had been keeping from me.

"Dude, I am so glad we won't have to take this class again at U of I."

I looked to Michael, who was busy shooting his friend one of those *thanks, bro* angry side eyes. U of I? He wasn't coming back? He was transferring? What in the real fuck?! We had finally broken through to the start of the rest of our lives together.

Michael asked his friend to leave and explained that he was indeed leaving Valparaiso at the end of the year, transferring to a new school, and here was the real kicker: He didn't see our relationship going any further.

Why had he brought me home? Why did he fight so hard to get me, then feel okay to let me go? It was an awful blow, and I felt pretty dumb for thinking I was going to marry this guy.

We went back to being friends, and I briefly learned a very valuable lesson: Not every man saw me like Leo had seen me. There is such a thing as just dating. I wish the lesson had stuck, but I still had my mojo and felt like it didn't have anything to do with a man giving it to me. Of all the labels I'd previously given myself—GOODY TWO-SHOES and PEOPLE PLEASER—SEXY GINGER was the most fun, the most empowering. Maybe the most "me," I thought.

A month after Michael and I broke up, I was raped. I am sorry if that sounds like it came out of nowhere. It is what the entire next chapter is about, and truly one of the most important and pivotal chapters in my developing identity. It is why SEXY GINGER took on a more distorted role. Promiscuity became a defense, a reaction to being a victim. What I thought was sexiness didn't always lead to great choices in partners. Over the next ten years, I would be drugged, have an abortion, and find myself in a horribly abusive relationship. I was often depressed and attempted suicide twice. The best form of SEXY GINGER did not stand a chance in this environment.

The abusive relationship with John, who I wrote about in my last book, took the last ounce of the pure SEXY GINGER. By the time I finally left John, every last drop of the confidence that being sexy had given me was destroyed. I was unmoored from myself, wondering if I even deserved to take up space on Earth. It's a miracle that my passion for meteorology, my ambition, and my human instinct to save my life and get away from an abuser motivated me to check myself into a mental-health hospital just ten days before I started at ABC.

After I got out of the hospital and began intense therapy twice a week, I finally began to find peace and the hope I'd almost given up on. It took a year before I felt safe enough to start dating Ben. But I still had issues with vulnerability and intimacy.

Thankfully, Ben had enormous patience and resolved to hang in there until I was ready to let him in. I've come a long way, but my sexuality still challenges me sometimes.

My husband will say that I am the sexiest woman he's ever met. But he has no idea what I used to be or what I know I am capable of. It's been almost a decade since I got out of the hospital, and I still feel like I'm crawling out of a well sometimes. When I met Ben, I'd given up being driven by lust, but I wasn't quite ready for the love Ben was offering. My relationship with Ben is unlike any I've ever had. It's based on respect, humor, and genuine heart-and-soul love. It's mature and sexy, but it's not yet the kind of sexy Val wanted me to bring to the samba.

HEALTHY, MARRIED GINGER is my new label. I'd love to find a way to bring SEXY GINGER back and integrate her into my life, but that isn't a simple task. Most of the time I feel like an asexual, self-pollinating tree. My husband is so kind and has never given me one moment to think he could harm me, but the history of abuse and trauma has constructed a wall that's hard for me to break down.

Before I married Ben, I was always on the hunt for men, my prey, scanning the room for my next target so I could move in like a cobra. When the thrill of the hunt was over and I finally addressed the traumas, my libido crashed. To get it back, I'd have to start the cycle over and over again.

Dr. Wilson says that there's an opportunity to find an even greater intimacy that goes well beyond the adrenaline of the hunt. I have always said that my love and respect for Ben were strong from the start, but the lust is the part that keeps growing. That's the beauty that marriage offers: When you give yourself over to one person completely, a sexual intimacy unfolds that is deeper and more meaningful than promiscuity.

So I don't expect to mirror my experience when I was nineteen, going back to a time before the wounds of my life; I just want to feel good in my body without any guilt or shame. I want to stand at the top of the stairs at Wrigley Field and spill beer all over my husband. He doesn't like baseball or beer, so he wouldn't really like that, but you get the point. I want him to feel that magic in me. 'Cause she's in there. SEXY GINGER 2.0—that's the goal.

CHAPTER TEN
"LIKELY" RAPE

In broadcast news, you learn early that you cannot make a claim, even when there is video evidence, that a crime is attached to a person. The word *allegedly* makes its way into scripts even when it sounds so wrong—because we can all clearly see that the crime happened, we know who did it, but we still can't say it until they are convicted. In this chapter, I will use the word *likely* before I use the word *rape*, not because I don't believe that I was raped, but because I can't prove it in a judicial way. This is one of those times when it sounds very wrong every time you read it, and that is intentional on my end.

I'll never drink Captain Morgan rum again. Ever. You hear people say it all the time. "I can't drink tequila because one time . . ." or "Vodka really affects me, as in makes me mean." Well, that's my relationship with the Captain.

It was the end of the second semester of my freshman year of college, and all my friends were planning to transfer, so this wasn't just the last hoorah our freshman year; it was the last party we would all have together ever. Michael and I were no longer dating, but we were close friends. He had moved on to a beautiful blond, and I was back together with Leo. There were farewell-to-school parties in almost every dorm room, but our group was doing the next-level blowout by starting a preparty in a room on the second floor of Alumni Hall. I lived on the fifth floor, so it was an easy jaunt down the stairs once I was ready. My prep for a party routine had become more elaborate now that SEXY GINGER was alive and well. I even wore foundation.

The music was so loud I could hear it as soon as I entered the fifth-floor stairwell. The thin wooden door was vibrating from the sound. I knocked but no one could hear me, so I slowly pushed down on the door handle to reveal a hidden oasis.

The room was not one I had spent much time in and I was impressed at how much work they had put into decorating it. There were lots of plants, posters, and they had stacked the beds to create a separate "living area" in the three-hundred-square-foot space. Very HGTV for freshmen in college.

Not thirty seconds after I walked in and started saying hello, someone handed me what smelled like a Captain and Coke in a red Solo cup. There must have been at least twenty people in that tiny space, and everyone was loud, dancing, and drunk already. I took a sip of my drink, trying to ease myself into the vibe of the party. I'd never had a drink this strong before but had come to think of myself as a "professional drinker" who could handle anything. Plus, I'd eaten a pretty big dinner, so I didn't think there would be any trouble. I started talking with a friend from one of my classes, asking him why he thought he and everyone else was so dead set on transferring. He sat in a deep chair, I was on the armrest, and that is the last thing I remember.

Until the next morning. The light from the window was bright, but I didn't have a headache. I felt foggy but not at all hungover.

I quickly realized I was naked. I clutched at the white sheet I was wrapped in and searched the room for my clothes. No clothes.

This was not my room. It was an empty dorm room, and I was on the bottom bunk of a bed.

School was officially over and the room had been stripped of everything, except me. I had no idea how long I'd been in this room, and I had no recollection of anything after the first few sips of that drink.

I rubbed my head, swung my feet to the cold tile floor, and slowly walked over to the bright light of the window. From the trees and the shape of the brick, I knew I was still in Alumni Hall. I just wasn't on my floor.

I wrapped the sheet around me and peeked out the door and down the hallway. I heard more voices than you typically would hear this early on a normal day. But this was move-out day and it wasn't that early. Students and their parents carrying boxes to the elevator thankfully left the stairwells relatively vacant. I ran down the hall and up the stairs to my room hoping that if anyone saw me, they would think they were seeing a ghost of a toga party rather than a shameful walk. I call it a shameful walk instead of a walk of shame because I really didn't know what had happened.

I was hoping my roommate would be able to fill in the blanks for me (she wasn't at the party the night before, but I was eager for clues), but when I got to our room, her parents were there helping her move out. She was one of the many students transferring next year—for her, back home to Wisconsin. My face flushed pink with embarrassment as her parents stared at me.

I mumbled a quick hello, quickly grabbed a T-shirt and some sweatpants, and left the room. I found some privacy in the shared bathroom down the hall and that's when I lost it. I sat on the floor of a shower with the yellowed shower curtain pulled shut tight as if that would close out the world, and bawled, trying to muffle my cries so no one would hear. When I couldn't cry anymore, I figured Kirsten and her family would be gone and I could safely go back to my room.

I sat on my bed praying for my memory to come back. I actually shut my door and got down on my knees on the side of my bed and prayed to God. I felt so helpless. With memory I could have fought the dark imagination that had filled my brain this past hour.

What if I had been drugged? What if I was raped? I mean it was possible, right? The more I thought about it, the more real it felt. Call it woman's intuition or my body giving me signals, but I just knew something really bad had happened to me. Women left naked in a room with no memory had been part of our freshman orientation warnings.

My mind started doing loops, and I was having a hard time breathing. I'd done my fair share of drinking this year and occasionally details would be fuzzy from the night before, but this was different. An entire night was gone!

Suddenly the phone rang. I was in no mood to talk to my parents or to Leo, but maybe it would be somebody who could help me figure out what happened last night. I picked up.

"Hello?" I said.

"Hey, y'all! This is WBMA ABC 33/40 in Birmingham, Alabama, calling."

The woman on the phone had a thick Southern accent. She sounded so friendly I thought maybe I was supposed to know who she was, but I didn't have a clue.

"I'm calling about the internship you applied for with

our weather department," she said. "Good news, you've been accepted!"

This woman had no idea she'd just saved my life. Who knows what I would have done if I'd be left alone with my fears much longer. This was great news, great enough to pull me out of my nightmare.

A few months before, I had applied for this internship, but I had totally forgotten about it because I really wasn't planning to go into television. I hadn't heard from any of the internships I had applied for (let's face it, who wants a fresh-man as an intern), so I had made plans to move back home and bartend at the club. I only applied to the TV internship because my professor told me he thought I would be good at it.

And in that very moment I had no doubt that I *needed* this internship in a state far away in a life I hadn't planned. I needed to make a change in order to run from what had likely happened. I needed something positive to help me for-get about that night.

I thanked the woman, and she gave me the details about when I started and what the job would entail.

When I hung up, I remembered my fear, which was now a conclusion, that I'd been raped. What was I supposed to do now? I couldn't go to the police because I wasn't 100 percent sure and had no idea who the perpetrator could have been. Plus, like a classic victim, I figured this was my fault. I shouldn't have had alcohol; I shouldn't have flirted with all those boys. I almost talked myself into a corner where I deserved to have this memory-less morning. I definitely couldn't make any of this known because what if my new bosses at my new internship found out? I could ruin my entire career if people found out SEXY GINGER had become SLUTTY GINGER. I figured the best course of action was to pretend it never happened.

I called Leo to give him the good news about my internship but mentioned nothing about the night before. I was his perfect princess and I needed him to still see me that way. He was so happy for me that I felt guilty all over again. I reminded myself: *Forget it—it never happened.*

I packed up all my things that afternoon and drove home. Within two weeks, Leo and I were on a road trip to Alabama. We rented an apartment and I loved my internship. I was excited about my life and determined not to look back. I kept my secret from Leo and avoided having sex with him until I could get a test in case I was carrying some kind of sexually transmitted disease. By the time we were in Alabama, I got the all clear and I fully pushed that night or rather that morning out of my mind. I just repeatedly told myself I was making it all up and nothing happened.

After the internship ended, we drove back to Michigan and promptly had to move back to our respective colleges to start our sophomore year. Within the first few weeks back at school, I noticed people whispering as I walked past. They would point then murmur to each other. Sometimes I would be around long enough or not quite far enough away and I would catch them giggling.

They were calling me a slut, a whore—all the names. I know this because I was a resident assistant that year, and some of my girls, once they got to know me well enough, felt comfortable asking. They asked me why people said I liked anal sex. I had never had anal sex, knowingly at least. And sometimes I learned that people on campus were referring to me as "the girl they ran a train on."

So, there it was. The answer to the question I had made myself forget and never really wanted the answer to.

Not only was I likely raped, but there may have been more than one person and it may have involved more than one part of me.

Anytime the thought came in my mind, I was still more powerful than it was. I would shake my head and say, "There's no way."

I was scared but I was tough, so I put it out of my mind and focused on my classes. And then I started having nightmares. Not just the normal scary nightmares where you can't wake up and shake them off. In these nightmares, I would wake up but I just couldn't move, and the nightmares would play out like a scary film transposed to my real life. I would find out later that this is called sleep paralysis and very common in people with narcolepsy, which I would soon be diagnosed with. But now I know it was also partly PTSD.

The nightmare would always start just like that night. I would see the image of myself sipping that drink and then, as if no time had passed, the nightmare would jump to an all-white room with me cowering on a bare bed. I would see a line of men in shadow coming toward me. I would beg them to leave me alone. Then, as if I had no voice and no strength, I would just lie there. I could feel them pressing down on me and I couldn't move. I couldn't get out.

I couldn't see their faces as they raped me.

And in sleep paralysis, I would "wake up" but I would still be in the nightmare. My body couldn't move. I essentially wakefully endured a rape.

My brain probably thought, *If you aren't ready to work through this while you are awake, I am going to get you while you are asleep.*

It felt like a memory more than my imagination, and there were mornings I put together a list in my head of the men most likely to have done this to me. As if I was ever going to confront them. Making things worse, there was nobody in my life I trusted enough to talk to and I was still so embarrassed, so I suffered alone in silence.

Over the years I told only three people about that night. It wasn't until I was in the hospital in New York City that I finally decided to be fully honest. And since then it has been a long road of working through and finding out how to unravel the web of psychological issues that evolve from something like that. That's probably the most healing I have had: *You don't have to remember it for it to have happened. You are allowed to grieve a "likely" rape, and it's definitely not your fault.*

I've read other accounts and scientific articles about drugged rape. According to *ScienceDirect*, about a quarter of victims never remember anything. About half remember intermittent details or have flashes of memory, and only 15 percent remember the rape in a "clear and concise" way.

Another *ScienceDirect* article made me realize it wasn't just me: "Victims usually report loss of memory during and after these incidents. They wake up at unfamiliar places, inappropriately dressed, and often with the sense but not the actual recollection of having had sex."

I wish the perpetrators of all sex crimes understood the consequences of their actions and the impact of those actions on their victims. In the years that followed my likely rape, I isolated myself from the friends I had and avoided making new ones. I made reckless choices with men, using my body as a weapon in what felt like an endless power struggle. But worst of all, I disconnected sex from love and refused to ever be that vulnerable college girl again. SEXY GINGER had gotten me in trouble, in my mind. I didn't want to be her anymore, so I tried to turn her off.

I wish I could go back to the morning after the rape and tell myself to go to the hospital and the police. I would make sure that there was absolutely no way this would impact my relationship with Leo or my future internship and career. I wish I really knew what happened so I could work through it.

Dr. Wilson and I have been talking about what impacts this event had on me. I have learned that the brain uses blocking as a defense, and that even if you are drugged, the memory is in there. Somewhere.

From the National Criminal Justice Reference Service I found this passage:

HOW DRUGGING IS A UNIQUE FORM OF TRAUMA.
Many of the difficulties victims face in the aftermath of these assaults are due to the effects of the drugs given by offenders. The surreptitious drugging of a victim is, in and of itself, a cruel and criminal violation of the person. Some victims describe this aspect of the trauma as "mind rape." The drugging should be recognized as a separate and distinct act of victimization in addition to any other acts of abuse and degradation to which the victim was subjected.

HOW BEING UNABLE TO FORGET COMPARES WITH BEING UNABLE TO REMEMBER.
In the aftermath of rape, most victims suffer acute stress disorder and post-traumatic stress disorder symptoms. One of the most disturbing symptoms is their inability to *forget* what happened. The trauma is reexperienced repeatedly.

> Victims commonly have recurrent, intrusive recollections of the rape, including thoughts, flashbacks, and nightmares. For victims of drug-facilitated rapes, this aspect of the aftermath may be experienced differently. Because they cannot *recall* what happened during a significant time period, they have to cope with a gap in their memory. They experience the horror, powerlessness, and humiliation of not knowing what was done to them. They can only imagine what happened. One victim said, "I would rather have the nightmare."

> https://www.ncjrs.gov/pdffiles1/jr000243c.pdf

I hope that my sharing of my experience will help other victims find the courage to tell someone. You did not ask to be drugged and raped. This is not your fault. Do not keep this to yourself. Find somebody you can talk to, and if you can, go to a hospital or to the police and help them find the criminal and bring them to justice. If it's been twenty years, as it's been in my case, you can and should still talk it out.

It's estimated that one out of every six women in America has experienced rape or attempted rape. Nine out of ten rape victims are women.

I still don't know for sure who raped me, or if it was indeed more than one person. But if you were involved and you're reading this book for some reason, I forgive you.

That forgiveness has not come easily, it was hard-won and a long time coming. I had to build myself up from the ground floor until I finally believed that I deserved to be happy, and that I'm the only one who can give or take away that happiness. Yes, you had the power that night, but I've finally taken it back. And I will use my platform to do whatever I can to give strength and hope to other victims and survivors.

Also, the other night I forced myself to take a sip of Captain Morgan rum because I wanted to not get over it but to work through it. I can happily report that I don't like it. Not because of the memory; I just think it's too sweet. The feeling that I am finally starting to move on is also sweet, but in a different way.

CHAPTER ELEVEN
MY FIRST MEDITATION

Sun-kissed in the early light of a summer Saturday in Oklahoma, Mount Scott and the towering rocks around it were glowing in majestic pinks, reds, and purples. I was in the Wichita Mountains Wildlife Refuge. It's a truly special place. In what is otherwise endless prairie land, this nearly sixty-thousand-acre refuge that escaped destruction because the soil was too rocky to plow, is now home to herds of bison, elk, deer, long-horned cattle, and hundreds of other protected animals. My sense of wonderment was extraordinary.

When I looked down, I noticed something that on any other day would not have even registered: a shallow puddle. I crouched down to get a closer look at the otherwise trivial divot in the land that allowed the recent rain to collect. But it wasn't trivial at all, it was intricate and complex, teeming with life.

Dozens of tiny water bugs were doing their thing, jumping

from side to side, swimming below the surface. They almost appeared to have a pattern they were following. Each one, I thought, had a name, a place in their bustling water-bug village. I sat in awe of the structure these insects were operating under. I sat for so long I even started imagining which little area was their post office or grocery store. The detail was surreal and comforting. I felt so connected to the little bugs because on a grander level, I believe there must be something or someone else looking down at humans on Earth with the same awe.

I would love to tell you that I came to this philosophical moment after years of studying meditation and Buddhism, or at that very moment in my late twenties I was having a breakthrough that would forever benefit my mental health.

Nope. I was hunched over, admiring a small pile of insects for an hour because I had just ingested a mason jarful of fermented cactus. I was on peyote.

Before you roll your eyes and think, *Oh goodness, she wasn't just abusing alcohol, it was drugs, too,* I swear on my children this was the only time I have ever experienced a drug grander than marijuana. And I don't regret it for a minute.

There is such beauty in this world. It's all around us. We just don't stop long enough to see it. You hear that constantly, but for the first time in my life, I was actually living it.

A little background. This was just months before my hospitalization. When a group of friends announced they would be meeting a shaman in the Wichita Mountains of Oklahoma, I said, "Why the heck not?"

I am not certain what I was expecting a shaman to look like. If I am honest, it would have been something more reminiscent of a monk perhaps? Instead, there was a guy who looked pretty much like a grad student who had taken a wrong turn trying to get back to campus. He lit some sage and walked us through what we could expect in the following eight hours.

Again, I had never experimented with drugs aside from a puff of a joint here or there (see, I know that a *puff of a joint* will tell you just how few times I have smoked), so I really had no base to go from. He told us there may be some mild digestive discomfort and then pure bliss. From his earthy-looking suede backpack he unwrapped several mason jars full of a thick dark greenish-brown liquid. He distributed a jar to each of us, waved the sage again, and disappeared after we had all gulped down the thick, mucous cactus guts.

The shaman suggested we hike into the mountains and experience this in nature, because it's not recommended to be in an urban or residential setting when you are about to trip for an entire day. If a pile of water bugs blew your mind, imagine seeing Elmo in Times Square.

I had been to those mountains before, and they were good for an easy hike and to take in some fresh American-plains air with a picturesque backdrop. The beginning of our hike felt very similar to the other times I had ventured into the Wichitas.

We had been hiking for ten minutes when one of the other women with us asked us all to slow down. She was feeling nauseous. She went behind a rock and started vomiting. Her boyfriend clutched at his lower intestines, obviously in pain. Another guy we were with started farting. It was all quite comical but a little scary, not knowing how long this part was going to last.

I just kept thinking, *Oh good, I am one of those that won't be getting the gastro impact.* But before that grateful thought even left my brain, I suddenly felt like someone had punched me in the stomach as hard as they could. I doubled over, crossing my arms and collapsing to the ground with a loud "Owww." I was in pain!!! But as quickly as it came on, it was gone. The gas passed and I was born again.

That's how it felt. I felt like I was being born into a new body and world. This new world was full of brilliant colors, euphoric feelings, and love-filled, blissful people everywhere.

We kept hiking for what felt like an hour before we came to the edge of a dazzling landing overlooking the valley below and more mountains in the distance. The red-clay colors of what is already a glorious landscape were made brighter and more vibrant by the drug. I really wish I could help Instagram create a filter for our pictures that would imitate the power of peyote.

Wow, what filter do you have on there?

Peyote.

Oh, love that one.

I don't think everyone needs to do peyote, but I really would love for all of you to be able to see and feel the world like I did that day. My mind was open.

The six of us sat independently, dozens of feet apart, yet we felt like we were holding hands and experiencing it all together. I got very focused on the mountains in the distance. While staring at them for what I am sure was thirty minutes but felt like three, I could see history, not just rock, jutting out from the land. There were three descending heights of rocks and as I stared, I realized they were telling me a story. The rocks looked undeniably like a horse with a man riding it and another man towering over them both with a gun and a sword. I could see the fear and strain in the horse's face. Tears started rolling down my cheeks and I began praying. It was so moving, and while I had known that story my entire life, it was touching me from the very ground that I sat on, because the peyote was allowing me to stay still, feel, and know it in my core.

From that spot, someone in the group got up enough motivation to keep hiking, so the rest of us followed. The day was perfect: low 70s, sunshine. We walked and stopped every few minutes. One of those stops was the water bugs, others were just long, deep breaths while watching the blue sky. One of the last stops, as the sun was setting, took us to the valley floor where dozens of trees stood, bare of leaves and surrounded by blackened sand. It was obvious a fire had recently blown through this part of the refuge. As I got in to take a closer look at the swirling black sands and dirt that encircled the trees, the landscape again transformed. This time it wasn't history but an art reference, the scene in front of me morphing into a Salvador Dalí creation. The twiglike trees became more cartoonish, like his tree in *The Persistence of Memory*. The surrealist painting came to life and I was walking through the oils, touching them and moving them like I was an artist within the art.

My invisible paintbrush started to lose its power, and that's when I knew my mind was closing and the drug was wearing off. We all started hiking out of the burned field of trees because it was almost dark and no longer safe for us to be tripping around. At dusk we were met again by the shaman who had stood watch over us the entire day (part of the package deal). We all started feeling our old selves again but were forever changed by the experience.

Fast-forward from that day to a few years later, when I met Dan Harris at ABC News. He had just written his life-changing book, *10% Happier* (coincidentally born from experimenting with cocaine, which led to a panic attack and then a deep dive into meditation). Dan introduced me to meditation as he has done for countless others. Sure, I had heard of it, but he explained it to me like no one else had. It is like a tread-mill for our mind. It will make us stronger. Stronger in mind is exactly what I needed in my life at that moment. I was going to therapy and finally learning my emotional-regulation tools, but this was another step I could do at home.

I read his book and gave it my all. I would sit, quietly, and try my best not to fall asleep (meditation may be more diffi-cult for narcoleptics, as a side note). Dan is a great coach. He kept assuring me that meditation is not about *thoughtlessness* but *thoughtful thoughts*. Our *monkey brains* as he calls them will forever be on the cycle of ping-ponging and running full speed, but meditation is the strength in allowing those thoughts to be just what they are: thoughts. Not acting on them, not writing them down. Just saying, *Okay, Ginger, that's a nice thought about how you need to look at peel-and-stick wall-paper, and yes, a nice thought about how Miles's bike helmet is getting too small. Nice thoughts. Nothing to do with them now. Let them go. They're just thoughts—let them go.*

You start to notice patterns about your thoughts and can start to almost anticipate them. This gives you control in your everyday life and not just that quiet moment on your cush-ion. For many people this settles them down. Their thoughts would often sweep them into a fury of anger or frustration. For me, meditation taught me how to drop in and feel. Settling and observing and not ignoring what I feel, thinking about what's happening around me. I really believe there is power in meditation, and I wrote a whole different chapter about this later in the book, about how it helped me work on my emotional regulation.

I certainly can't do peyote every day, but in some of my most meditative moments I have felt a glimmer of the same euphoria. My mind has been open enough, and I have the Wichita Mountains to aspire to.

The best part? After all the stories were told that night back in Oklahoma as we drove home, the shaman asked, "How far do you think you hiked?" We all guessed two to ten miles. I thought it had to be somewhere close to six miles at least. He informed us we had barely made it in a quarter-mile loop outside the parking lot. All that beauty, all that open-mindedness is right in front of us. That's what I never let go from my experience that day.

With our blinders on, we run full-steam ahead doing twenty miles only to have not seen a damn thing along the way. Sometimes you can do less to see more. Just take the blinders off—there are some water bugs that need your attention.

CHAPTER TWELVE
THE CHOICE

A reminder: This book is about healing. I had just gotten my "big break" for my first full-time TV job. I packed up my car and moved across the state to start work at WEYI in Clio, Michigan. I'd been dreaming about being a broadcast meteorologist since that fortuitous phone call in college (prior to that, my plan was to be Helen Hunt in *Twister*). I have always been extremely ambitious, so I probably put even more pressure on myself to succeed. And I didn't just demand success in my new career, I wanted it in my personal life at the same time. According to NATURAL DISASTER GINGER, this was the perfect time to buy my first house, hopefully get engaged, and be a productive member of society. A young woman with tens of thousands of dollars in college debt, a car payment, and a contract that would pay just barely above minimum wage thought a mortgage would be a good idea. Sounds like an unbalanced equation, right? It gets worse.

The house was a charming 1950s ranch style, two bedrooms on a corner lot in Flushing, Michigan. It was a picturesque suburban oasis on the outside, but on the inside, it was the opposite of "turn-key" and more "Run away, run away now. Please don't buy this endless abyss of impossible renovations." Not quite as bad as the house in the Tom Hanks movie *The Money Pit*, but pretty darn close. Every room needed work. The bathroom had Pepto-Bismol–pink tile; the living room had an Asian-inspired wallpaper appliqué on lime-green walls with built-in planters. The house needed a new roof, new flooring, new windows, and a new septic system. See, there was a super-special amenity that was not mentioned in the listing: Every time we had a heavy rain, the Flint River would rise and my septic tank would back up into my basement, flooding it with literal shit. Making my house a literal shit box.

That basement, when not flooded with feces, was the perfect entertaining space. The tile floor had built-in games like hopscotch and shuffleboard, every wall was dark cherrywood like a cabin, and the centerpiece was a sixteen-foot wet bar. I dreamed of the parties Jake and I could throw once we were playing house on Circle Drive. See, he was a big part of the "perfect life" equation. I assumed Jake would want to move in and lend a hand in the repairs, ask me to marry him, and take long walks with me and my black Lab, Otis. But he was twenty-three, had a new job, and owned a home of his own.

Between my ridiculous expectations, the distance, and our age, our relationship wasn't in great shape, and we broke up within the first few weeks of me being in Flint.

With extra time on my hands now, I decided to focus on the rehab. The neighborhood gossip was that my house was haunted by a woman named Rose and her former husbands (apparently the name Rose was the reason for the abundance of pink paint and tile, and yes, there were many husbands according to neighbors). Despite the potential for several ghosts and the grease-drenched cabinets that had to be scrapped because of Rose's fifty-year deep-frying addiction, I loved my house. My dog had a yard and I felt like a grown-up every night I walked in the door. My parents were helping out with the big remodeling projects, so they were around every other weekend. But on the off weeks when they weren't with me, and during the weekdays, the newness wore off and I was lonely. Playing shuffleboard alone, even after consuming an entire box of wine, is not a great time.

I was enjoying my job, but I hadn't made any friends yet. One night my coworkers invited me to hang out with them at a tiki bar near my house, and I saw this as a great opportunity to introduce them to FUN GINGER.

The bar had giant palm fronds, real sand, and tiki tables. For Flint, Michigan, it was an island oasis in the desert of Applebee's and Chili's. When I walked in, I saw a few of the newly familiar faces. They waved me over to an empty seat at the bar, and since I was sophisticated now, I ordered a dirty martini. Extra dirty. That had been my new go-to drink ever since Christina Aguilera had recently released my favorite song, "Dirty." Leave it to me to connect sophistication to an artist who wears chaps in a boxing ring.

The martini showed up not in a beautiful glass like we would have served it in at the club, but in a flimsy plastic cup with two small green olives sans pimento or blue cheese. Despite the lack of beverage perfection, this really felt like the ideal summer night in mid-Michigan.

I remember having a funny conversation with a few coworkers about my obsession with John Cusack and drinking the rest of my martini. But that's it. When I woke up the next morning, I was naked and there was vomit on my new white duvet cover. It was already 9 a.m., so Otis really needed to go out and wouldn't stop nudging the bed. I got up and everything about me felt awful. And embarrassed. I could not remember anything and I hadn't even had a second drink. At least, I didn't think I had.

What was extra strange: my car wasn't in my driveway. That made me feel better because the last thing I would ever do is drive drunk. My keys were in my purse, so I took Otis for a two-mile walk back to the bar, where I hoped my car would be. At least it wasn't that far because I had no idea who

I would have called to get a ride. This was long before Uber, and the Yellow Pages did not have a substantial section for taxis in Flint. Once I pulled into my driveway, still searching my brain for some inkling of a memory, I got distracted by my messy garage and started organizing. Task after task kept me busy without allowing idle time for thinking because a big part of me wanted to pretend that last night had not happened. After hydrating and getting some food in me, I went for a run and had almost shaken the fuzzy feeling by the time I got in the shower to get ready for work.

Hanging my head in shame, I was mortified that my big opportunity to present myself to my coworkers as FUN GINGER turned into a wild night with a version of myself I had only met once before: DRUGGED GINGER. Or at least I thought. You would think that after that first experience I would have some idea of what to do. It had been just over three years.

I was a serial monogamist and my flirtations always had a purpose. I never had sex with someone I didn't know. I had never had a fling, never a one-night stand. Even in my drunk moments, I had kissed people but never went home with them or had them come to my place.

After my "likely" rape in college, I wielded sex as a weapon, but always required the promise of monogamy. On the guys' part at least. I did a lot of what I liked to call "crossover," when, toward the end of one relationship, I would cross over to another guy before I had fully broken it off with the last one. Like a monkey that goes from vine to vine to avoid falling below the treetops, I used the crossover to avoid falling into the pool of lonely singles.

My MO was to trap them, make them commit to calling me their girlfriend, then have sex. So, having a one-night stand made no sense.

Then I did what I do best. I ignored it and pretended it never happened and hoped no one asked any questions. I had expertly avoided this very same situation in college so I felt confident I could bury it and move on.

Just over a month later, I got the opportunity to substitute for our morning show meteorologist. I woke up with genuine excitement that Monday at 2:30 a.m. I loved getting to fill in on the weekday shows and prove what a strong meteorologist I was becoming. I sat up ready to take on the day and a wave of nausea took over my body. I swallowed and quickly made my way to the kitchen for some water. Once I felt a little less sick, I hurried to the shower, and when the water was warm enough, I stepped in and let it wash over me, hoping that would erase the last bit of pukey feeling.

The dizziness was quickly replaced by severe pain in my boobs and nipples. Like someone was taking little scalpels and scraping them over and over with every drop of water. *What a strange sensation,* I thought, and I got dressed for work.

But when the second round of nausea hit at 5 a.m. and I could not ignore my boobs throbbing any longer, I grabbed my planner and did the math. Crap. My period was five days late. I had been on the pill since I was sixteen. I always took my pill at the exact same time, as I had been educated about the importance of keeping the hormone consistent for best efficacy. So this could not be real.

Moments later, I started our two-hour morning show followed by two more hours of *Today* show cut-ins, knowing that I must be pregnant.

As soon as I finished my last segment I ran to the nearby Walmart and bought a pregnancy test. I had at least an hour before the producers would notice that I was gone and before we started prepping for the noon show. I made it back with forty-five minutes to spare. I slammed the car door and strode into WEYI. I tried to conceal the plastic Walmart bag in my purse just in case I ran into anyone on the short jaunt from the front door to the bathroom.

I shoved open the swinging door and chose the stall farthest away. I could not believe I was taking a pregnancy test five months into my first real job. This made my forgetting my shoes and wearing flip-flops for the first week, and not knowing who Tiger Woods was (all in *Natural Disaster*) look like child's play.

There is no way, I thought as I peed on the stick. Within seconds, the display screen filled in.

It was positive.

My initial reaction was to clutch the pee stick with the telltale two lines as I gasped with what I can only describe as joy. I had always wanted to be a mother. Tears began to flow down my face, but the reason for the tears shifted quickly. Tears are an auto response of the body after it reaches an unsafe level of arousal—positive or negative. It's our body's effort to equalize. My arousal quickly changed from elation to deep fear.

I dropped the stick on the floor of the dirty TV-station bathroom. Reality hit. The tears turned to heaving and I threw up.

I couldn't have this baby! I had just started my career. I was living alone three hours from my parents in a house with a bum septic tank and a bad roof. I couldn't tell my parents I was pregnant. The jumps from SEXY GINGER to DRUGGED GINGER to PREGNANT GINGER were happening far too quickly for me to process. There was no way my family, friends, or my new bosses and viewers would be able to handle this shock.

For all my parents knew, I was still with Jacob. If this was Jake's baby, it might have been a different story. . . . And I was on the pill! I was actively trying to prevent this from happening. (Note: I would later find out that my narcolepsy medicine was making my birth control ineffective.)

I grew up Lutheran and God did not allow for abortion. Did he? I had always prided myself on being so careful and protective of my hopes and dreams. This was not supposed to happen. This only happened to careless people! My mind was cluttered with questions and doubts, every emotion on the spectrum. Damn you, Christina Aguilera! Just kidding, I still love that song. Plus, it was also Redman's fault if we are really placing unjust blame on an early 2000s song.

It had to be the tiki bar night. I walked out of that bathroom with no idea what to do, so I just went on TV, feigning interest in the high and low temperatures and showing the chances of precipitation.

As I am writing this, I realize I haven't thought about that moment in so long. Now that I have learned to allow myself to be honest, I can say confidently that in that first week I was really considering having the baby. A big part of me wanted to.

Here's where I went wrong. I didn't tell my friends, nor my mom or dad. I kept going back and forth in my mind alone. It was eating me alive.

This is the part that really upsets me about my choice. I had never felt confident enough in listening to my gut. I always sought out other opinions, but in this case, I was too ashamed to even ask. I worried what others would think or feel, so I never asked anyone. And that drove me to make a choice that I don't think I really wanted to make. My heart was saying yes, have this baby. But my brain was so full of what it would mean to my career and what it would mean for this child's life. Could I even have a career if I was a single mother? I thought, *Maybe I will just get an ultrasound.*

The next day I got an appointment at my doctor's office. The ultrasound tech congratulated me and I sat there nodding, not sure what to say. I had come to find out my options, and this woman only saw one option. Before I could say anything, the lights were down and the cold lubricant around the vaginal ultrasound stick was inside me. And there, on the screen, was what looked like a circle within a peanut. She told me that that was the baby and I was likely seven to eight weeks pregnant. She then turned the volume on. And there it was. The heartbeat.

Bya bum, ba bum, ba bum.

I started to cry. The doctor came in and the ultrasound tech had obviously conveyed my less than joyous reaction. My doctor asked if my husband would be with me next time and told me I should come back in a month to do another ultrasound. Abortion was never mentioned and I felt too ashamed to ask. I didn't even say that I didn't have a husband because that part felt shameful in this room, too.

I drove back to my house in a fog. All I could think about was trying to get the baby out of a car seat, not sleeping, working the morning shift, paying for a babysitter with money I didn't have. College debt, a mortgage, and my car payment were constantly looming and forcing me to substitute teach and bartend. My boss at the station wasn't a huge fan of mine even before something as shocking as this; I couldn't imagine how she would have reacted had I been a young woman on TV, unmarried and pregnant. How different this would have been even today, when being married is far less socially crucial and even having children out of wedlock is not nearly as taboo as it used to be.

All that said, being a parent even today changes the way people look at you in the workplace. That's something I wish we could alter, because having a family or children, no matter how and when this comes to you in life, should be celebrated, if it's something you want. That's not how it works, as we have learned during the pandemic when four times the number of women dropped out of the workforce than men after childcare systems collapsed. Even pre-pandemic, young children were the cause of joblessness in women because of caretaking responsibilities. Women with at least one child under the age of six were more likely to report caretaking (61 percent) as the reason they experienced joblessness than women with children ages six to seventeen only (46 percent).

Over the next few days, I spiraled into a combination of depression and anxiety. Amid the massive changes that were happening to my body, my mind was all over the place.

After a few more days, I knew I couldn't do it. I was putting more value on the career I had worked so hard for already. No part of me felt like I could have both, and no part of me really wanted to raise a child without a solid, loving base of a family I did not have. That was the part that really swayed me. Why would I want a child to come into this world without having the "ideal" two-parent unit that I so desperately yearned for?

When I arrived at the clinic, the building was far from impressive—a brick, one-story edifice with bars on the windows. The waiting room was large, but there were only two other people in it. After I reluctantly checked in, it was only minutes before they called my name to come beyond the glass-block wall that separated the waiting room from, by the sound of it, what had to be a giant vacuum.

Once I walked into the room, they weighed me, checked my blood pressure, asked a few questions, asked me to take my bottoms off, and within a few minutes the IV was in.

I eased onto the cold, hard white hospital sheet over the gurney and stared up at the overhead light.

And just that fast, the anesthesia took hold. I was still so conflicted in those last wakeful moments, thinking I could still get out. Societal fear and a willingly accepted anesthesia were holding me down this time. I wanted to yell, *Wait! I'm not sure . . . Maybe I could make this . . .*

And then I woke up. And I immediately knew there was no more choice. It was over and that group of cells with a heartbeat, my baby, was gone.

I came to in a holding room, sitting upright in a chair. I

was magically holding a cup of sweet tea in one hand and a cookie in the other. The sugar was meant to bring my blood sugar up enough to make me feel better after the procedure.

A waterfall of tears began rolling down my face.

I looked up and saw more tears around the room. I wasn't alone. It was like a horrible episode of *Black Mirror* where everyone's feelings were being evoked at the same time. I don't think I had been anywhere this sad, ever.

My mind started racing, thinking about how these other women came to this same room at the same time. Were they raped? Incest? Abusive husband? Then I realized it didn't really matter what circumstance got them here; they didn't want to have had to make this choice.

And that was it.

When I emerged from the post-op room to the waiting room, I saw the clock. Only thirty minutes had passed.

That's all it took.

Thirty minutes and my entire life changed forever.

A nurse handed me a maxipad and warned that the bleeding would be heavy over the next twenty-four hours. That's it. No explanation about how I might feel, where to get help if I felt depressed, no warning about the intense drop in hormones that women go through after an abortion. Just a big maxipad.

The guilt and shame were erupting and I needed support. Jacob joined me in my home as I mourned. He didn't ask questions, he just hugged me. Jake was always my safe space. I fell asleep crying. I did not know that that many tears could be produced from one person.

I woke up numb the next morning. It was Halloween 2003. My eyes were almost swollen shut from crying so much the day before. The nurse was right: the bleeding was bad. I had bled right through my sheets. As I loaded the washing machine to try to erase the abortion from my mind, like I would hopefully catch the bloodstain before it set, I felt a twinge of warmth when Otis settled at my feet. But uncharacteristically I asked Otis to go away.

The numbness was giving way to darkness. Jake was so fearful and tender, tiptoeing around, trying to artfully figure out if we just go on like nothing happened or talk and talk and talk about something we could no longer do anything about.

The doorbell rang and I opened the door slowly, still feeling weak. There stood a little toddler dressed as a cow.

"Twick or tweet."

I stared at him for five long awkward seconds, didn't give him any candy, closed the door, and slowly turned around and crumpled to the floor. I didn't have any more tears. Jacob shut off the lights so no more trick-or-treaters would ring the bell and then he carried me to bed.

The next morning, Jake suggested I go back with him to

Grand Rapids for a few days. He had to get back to work and I knew he was scared to leave me alone. I think I was scared of being alone, too, so I agreed. I had called in sick for the weekend because I thought I would be bleeding too badly.

I don't remember the drive home that day, but I drove my own car, following Jake to his house. We ate dinner at our favorite spot in Grand Rapids and I felt another wave of guilt wash over me.

Throughout the weekend, the blinds of depression kept closing. By Sunday night, my mood was closing in on what I had felt less than a year before when I tried to take my own life. I figured a good night's sleep would help.

The next morning, Jake set me up in his bedroom, gave me a kiss on the cheek, and promised to be home by dark. He turned around before he left to look at me and said, "I love you."

I smiled. And returned, "I love you, too."

But at that moment, I didn't mean it. Nothing mattered that morning except one thing.

I had woken up with one plan and one plan only for November 3, 2003. To take my own life.

I didn't have a question. I did not want to live. The blinds of depression that I had felt closing earlier slammed shut and there was not a sliver of light. There was just no way I could ever forgive myself or heal.

As soon as I heard Jake's car pull away, I got up from under the blankets, put on jeans, a top, and a coat that was far too light for the autumn chill that had settled in. Otis and I hopped in my Eclipse, and I drove as fast as I could to the pharmacy.

I remembered that after my first suicide attempt the nurse had said, "Thank goodness you didn't take more Tylenol. Tylenol is the one that can really shut down a liver."

So Tylenol it would be. I paced the aisles looking for the Tylenol when the sign above it caught my eye: PAIN RELIEVERS. I took the supersize bottle meant for years of pain relief in hopes that it would indeed relieve my pain. Forever.

As I was checking out, I added a pack of Marlboro. Not even light. I was a closet smoker and figured I might as well go out hard. I had this strange sense of joy briefly when I thought about this person selling me this and not knowing it was for me to take my life. Like this was my secret. Kind of like the anorexia pizza-in-the-milk-carton moment. But on a much grander scale.

I drove to a public park, let Otis out to run and play, and sat on a bench. I barely thought about it. I just started taking the pills by the handful and washing them down with a giant bottle of water.

I am not a great pill taker, so this was a challenging feat. Midway through, I thought for sure I was going to throw up just from attempting to ingest this much this quickly.

But I didn't. I finished the whole thing, lit a cigarette, and stared at the horizon blankly. I thought it would only take a few minutes. I expected to fall down immediately, hoping everything would go black.

But that didn't happen. Nothing happened. So I lit another cigarette. And another. I think I smoked at least half a pack. When I still didn't feel anything, I had time to realize I hadn't really thought this whole thing through and decided I didn't want to be found dead in a park, so I drove back to Jake's.

It was remarkable to me how normal I felt.

I was antsy, waiting for something to happen, so I flipped on the TV to pass the time. My mom called when I was watching an episode of *Fresh Prince*. She knew nothing about the abortion or the hundreds of pills floating in my stomach, but she knew I wasn't doing great mentally. She could tell from my visit over the weekend. I told her I was fine, but I guess she didn't believe me because she insisted on seeing for herself. She picked me up at Jake's house, and we went shopping at Burlington Coat Factory, The Limited, and Ann Taylor.

When I try to describe to someone what the deepest depression was like for me, I can now use this example. I cared so little about my life, about anything, I acted like absolutely nothing was happening when I was being poisoned slowly by my own choosing—right in front of my mom. I smiled and laughed with her so that she would let me go, so I could die in peace. Whenever I shined brightest, it was usually my mask of depression thickening. And this was elite-level performance masking numbness and depression.

When she was satisfied with my mood, my mom dropped me back at Jake's. As soon as I got back, I tore off "the mask" and jumped into Jake's bed. Shaking, crying, and gasping for air, I was starting to feel the Tylenol. My body felt hot and I started vomiting. I was scared now.

I heard the door open. Jake was home early. He ran upstairs and I pulled the blanket over my face.

He came to hug me, holding a bag that smelled so bad.

"I brought you Taco Bell! Bet you haven't eaten all day."

As soon as I saw the bean burrito, I threw up again. But this time it was green. Bright green. It was bile.

When I couldn't stop and Jake saw blood in the bile, he said we were going to the hospital.

I begged him not to.

He dragged me into the car. At first he was thinking it was a side effect of the abortion. Then he figured it out.

"What did you do, Ginger? What did you take?"

The whole way to the hospital, I refused to tell him it was Tylenol. When I started vomiting again in front of the ER, they begged for the truth. I figured they knew I did something, so I reluctantly gave it up. I was so angry that my suicide attempt didn't work. I had failed, again.

The nurses rushed me into a room, but it turns out Tylenol

is not lethal right away; it can take days for your liver to fail. They gave me an IV of a trial drug that was relatively new to the US but had been used in Europe. It flushed my liver without having to pump my stomach. I was going to be fine.

Not long after, my mom and Carl walked in. Moments later, my dad.

I shot my mom a look—she knew I was not pleased that my dad was in the room. I hated being imperfect in front of anyone. Especially him.

"I had to call him. We didn't know if you were going to make it. He deserves to be here."

As embarrassed as I was to be in this place for a second time in my adult life, seeing my mom's petrified eyes, it got infinitely worse.

A nurse came in.

"Ginger, your blood levels are improving, but we checked everything else and you are pregnant."

She said that in front of everyone.

My parents all looked at me, then looked at Jake and back at me.

I just stared at the nurse.

"No, I'm not. I was, but I'm not anymore. I had an abortion."

They were all in shock. My mom dove in and started hugging me, telling me she wished I had come to her, that she was so sorry we had to go through this alone. We. They definitely thought it was Jake's baby. We didn't correct them. We just all sat there crying.

I didn't think I deserved their compassion. I was so angry I hadn't succeeded in taking my own life.

Years later, a therapist attributed my suicide attempt, in part, to the hormonal drop that occurs after an abortion. There's no question that the hormones exacerbated the hopelessness. I think that's an important factor, and obviously I wish I'd been warned about it, because I think it's risky to leave out the emotional component of an abortion for some women.

Even without the hormone drop, I think I would have felt the same deep levels of shame and guilt. This is not uncommon, but it's not talked about enough. Abortion is an extremely complex subject, and that doesn't mean we should limit conversations to morality, religion, and politics. It's far from a black-and-white issue.

More than anything, abortion is a personal decision, and women deserve compassion, not judgment. I had to make the decision of my life within a couple of weeks. If I had felt less shame for being pregnant, if I had felt like I could have a career as a single mom . . . if, if, if.

If I'd had an IUD, everything might have been different. The pill isn't perfect. The IUD is nearly perfect and can have innumerable benefits, from having the lowest direct dose of hormones to protecting me from endometrial cancers.

I wish more women had access to protection like the IUD so they'd never have to consider abortion. An IUD gives you an actual choice. *You.* Not anyone else, not alcohol, drugs, or a violator. It gives *you* the choice.

But for those of you who do find yourself pregnant and having to make a choice, don't do it alone. There's so much power that comes from talking to another person. There's a saying in 12-step programs: "You're only as sick as your secrets." Although I'm not in the program, I very much believe this is true.

Jacob and I broke up for good that spring, and I focused on my career. The shameful, dark secret was buried, and I never let myself work through it or mourn my loss.

Instead, I ran away, constantly trying to make up for what I had done in an escalated quest for perfection in my personal life.

That secret was a big reason I said yes too soon to a proposal just over a year later from a sweet man whom I'd known for only six months. A man I would crush by running away three weeks before our wedding. The spiral from the college rape to the abortion to the runaway-bride situation did not set me up for personal life success.

It's taken a long time and a lot of therapy to even talk about this. I am still embarrassed. I am still in pain. But I have seen the benefit of sharing my other stories—it always helps someone. I hope this story does that, too. I know many of you will never look at me the same way. And that's okay. I have embraced it and I am ready because I know this could help another woman.

Now I allow myself to mourn for the child that could have been because of that secret. The child I will never know. She would be seventeen now, and I'd probably be talking to her about sex and protection. She'd be a teenager, making my life a challenge, but she'd also be a big sister to my little boys. In my mind she is a girl. Although I don't think there is any way I could have really known, I just knew.

I can't go back and change what I did, but I can finally thank my baby for what she gave me: the ability to forgive myself. My hope is that no matter what secret trauma or pain you might be holding on to, you open it back up, work on it, and eventually find peace with it. This is why I wrote this book. Without sharing this story and being honest about this part of my life, I would not really be managing my mental health.

I want this chapter to be her legacy. I am not telling people whether or not they should get an abortion. Your body, your choice. I just wish for a societal shift. Less secrecy, more understanding, more support, and more emphasis on prevention.

CHAPTER THIRTEEN
OH YEAH

My brother and I proudly yelled the lyrics to the Ghost-busters song while circling the couch after seeing the film for the first time.

It had to be 1986. I was five; he was almost three.

I was developing my FEARLESS GINGER persona.

If you look at my adventure résumé, you would probably call me fearless. I've paraglided in the Andes, the Himalayas, and the southern Rockies. I have been hang gliding, rock climbing, ice boat racing, and spent a week in a cave only three hundred people had been in before, exploring cliffs and parts of our planet not yet touched. When I saw my first tornado, I didn't feel fear; I felt curiosity. When I sat on the edge of the open plane door about to do a live skydive on *GMA*, my thoughts went to what I should have had for breakfast because I was still hungry. In many ways, I guess I *am* fearless.

But now that I have taken the time to uncover what I really have been doing to succeed in all of these stunts, I think I might not be so fearless after all.

When I first moved to Chicago, I lived in one of the giant towers that held hundreds of apartments at the end of Randolph Street on Lake Michigan. The views were unparalleled, the apartments and the amenities were dazzling, and they even had a grocery store on the lowest level. It was also about $500 a month over my budget, which I had erroneously calculated going into my new gig at WMAQ.

The building was in an area that was still developing. Years after I left, shops and restaurants and a really refined river walk were put in. When I lived there, it was a bit of a construction site, and even though I could see the NBC tower when I exited my building, you had to navigate an underground labyrinth of tunnels and that not-yet-developed, rudimentary river walk to get to a bridge to go up the metal stairs, cross the bridge, and walk north to the building.

That was one of the big reasons I kept my car at first. With my early-morning hours, it wasn't a great idea to be walking the underground of the city at 3:30 a.m. on a Saturday or Sunday. So I would get in my Mitsubishi Eclipse, blast some party music, and drive the five minutes of twists and turns to the garage at NBC.

Once I realized the rent was just never going to work, I found an apartment in Lakeview right outside Wrigley Field that I shared with a new friend. One sunny day in the Windy City, I got a message from my old building that they had my security deposit to return, but I had to pick it up in person. I had just finished up at work and decided to walk over there.

By this point I had only done this walk once or twice, and it made me uncomfortable. I was normally able to control this type of fear. I learned to identify "real" things and "fake" things from my dad. He would let us watch horror movies at a very young age. I had a bunch of my first-grade buddies over and we watched *Friday the 13th* since my birthday was on Friday the thirteenth. I am sure those poor girls are still scarred. Whether it's horror or sexual content or violence, there is a reason that there are guidelines (albeit a little conservative in some cases, I think) for children. My dad let us watch any movie, any show, no matter the rating. He always took the time to explain if he saw us getting scared or uncomfortable.

"Ging, this is only a movie. It's not real. Don't worry," he would say.

That was reassuring enough for me, and I developed a sort of tool kit to block out the fearful emotions I would feel while I was watching movies. What's interesting is that I never once thought of what this meant in real life. I don't love horror movies—not because they scare me, but because I really see them as so fake, I can't even drum up the fear. But it turns out that it's another case of me not allowing my emotions to surface. Like Elsa says, "Conceal, don't feel."

My dad had been taught to suppress emotion. And while he never once said that I should do this in real life, too, I made the connection and started doing it with real emotions.

The summer I fell in love with weather was a stormy one on Lake Michigan and my cousins were staying with us. I was nine years old and we watched two movies that summer: *The Goonies* and *Cocktail. Cocktail* has some intense romantic scenes, and I remember feeling the emotions start to build and immediately knew what to do: I shut them down.

I used to wonder why young kids shrink in embarrassment watching an on-screen kiss. I assumed it stemmed from seeing something sexual while they were in the same room as their parents. Turns out, it's not that simple. My son, Adrian, is four and he turns away or plants his face in a pillow anytime a man and woman are even interested in each other on-screen. My husband and I haven't been as lenient as my dad was with movies, but we have certainly pushed the age restrictions. Take *Weird Science*, a favorite of Ben's. It's relatively benign, but there are boobs and innuendo throughout the film. I was really surprised to see Adrian turn his head and look into the pillow even during some of the more sophisticated humor or innuendo. He was understanding it and just couldn't watch.

Dr. Wilson said that isn't embarrassment; it's a child not knowing what to do with that level of arousal of emotion. It's too much for them. When this happens now, I make sure to ask Adrian how he is feeling and why he is feeling that way. We have also backed off a bit and are sticking with *Dennis the Menace* and animal documentaries (which come with a whole different set of questions, but those are a little easier to process because the characters aren't human).

In the 1980s, my parents would never have been in tune with psychology enough to ask me what I was feeling. My mom avoided showing my brother and me anything, and my dad just told us to stuff that emotion down.

The first time a movie made me cry I was ten years old. I was alone at my dad's house on a Saturday (my dad and Pam must have been at Sean's wrestling match) and I couldn't wait to see it. Macaulay Culkin with that bright smile and Anna Chlumsky holding her forehead laughing on the VHS cover at Blockbuster made me reach for the film.

I settled into my dad's recliner because I never got to sit in that chair when everyone else was home. The low winter-afternoon sun was still coming through the windows when I squeezed the plastic sleeve to let the VHS tape emerge. *My Girl*. I put it in the VCR and settled back into that chair.

Perhaps it was because no one else was around and there was no need to tamp down any emotion. Or maybe it's because Brian Grazer and Howard Zieff had made a beautiful, simple film about a boy and a girl close to my age. But, spoiler alert, when Macaulay Culkin's body is shown in that casket, my throat tightened. I knew this feeling but hadn't had it many times in my life. It was the feeling I got before I cried. It scared me as one tear rolled down my cheek. I sat there, shocked that I was crying at a movie. I had heard of people doing this but not anyone close to me. My family watched mostly comedy and action films anyway, so there was no real place for crying. Another tear followed and I felt a rush of emotion and, oddly, relief. I had allowed my emotion to build instead of shoving it down, and it snuck out. I felt oddly ashamed.

The tears started to dry and the credits rolled. I kept the credits going and went to pee, leaving the door open so I could watch the very end. I thought this was a magical movie. It had actually made me feel. But I couldn't tell if I liked that feeling or hated it. It felt difficult. Like a confrontation between my mind and body. I liked controlling my feelings. I had just recently started controlling my weight, and it had become my favorite pastime. I vowed right there and then to never tell anyone about those tears.

From then on, if *My Girl* was suggested for a sleepover, I would say, "*My Girl* just isn't good. It's cheesy." In reality, I didn't want to feel again.

It's amazing how long that practice has been going on inside me. Almost thirty years. It has allowed me to do some pretty spectacular things without the fear, anger, and sadness others feel. But it has also caused great grief for me as well.

When the cheerleaders at my school made it to state finals for the first time in our school's history, my teammates cried with joy, but I remained stoic. I was proud, but I never let that energy build up and release. Six years of dedication, broken limbs, stitches, and love for a sport. I never let that get the best of me, even when it culminated in an invitation to the top competition.

Similarly my nerves didn't take over in my sonatina festivals when playing piano. Or before the SAT or ACT tests. As I think back, it's likely that my expertise at flatlining my emotions was a perfect companion to the narcolepsy I was developing. With narcolepsy, you're never fully awake. A pattern for sure.

Going back and forth between my parents' houses those first few years between ages seven and twelve had a profound effect on me. My mom's undiagnosed and unmedicated chemical imbalances manifested in explosive behavior on at least a weekly basis. The unpredictability was so hard to be around and to process as a kid. And then Sean and I didn't have anywhere to safely go to express how that made us feel. So my brother and I probably both used that tool of concealing, not feeling. It's much easier and safer—at least in the moment. My mom was always sorry for her outbursts, but it was impossible to have a fully open and safe line of communication with her.

And I never felt comfortable enough to call my dad and say that Mom was scaring me, and I didn't know how to help her. Of course I didn't know. I was eight years old. And no one was there to help me. But I had to be strong for Sean. We used humor to get through it. Even now, I am writing through glasses fogged from the tears that are rolling down my face. Thirty years of built-up emotion tends to leak out.

When my stepdad, Carl, came into our lives, I didn't feel safe enough or know him well enough to seek emotional support from him. Not at all his fault and he did what he could. He created a shield for Sean and me, and it was a huge relief to have another adult present, not only to witness my mother's blowups but to assure us and her that her behavior was not appropriate. Carl would usher her outside as soon as he could. He was protecting Sean and me and, best of all, supporting and helping her.

As my skill at concealing and not feeling was honed through my teens, I started wearing it like a badge of honor. Proud to be the tough one, the one who could handle anything. Even when boyfriends started saying I was detached, I just accepted that that is who I was innately. It wasn't until I started writing this book that I started diving into the truth about my feelings. Allowing emotions to erupt and be. Meditation seems to be working the opposite way for me than it does for most people. Instead of learning not to be swept away by emotions and to find my "calm," I was learning to wake up and feel the emotions.

There's an analogy I came up with recently that's been very helpful.

In the first few years at GMA I often worked fourteen to thirty days straight without a day off. Because I loved the work so much and was so excited about the opportunity to do network television, I didn't mind a bit. My usual travel itinerary would be to leave Sunday nights after *World News Tonight*, be on the road for GMA Monday through Friday, then return to New York for the weekend shows. Traveling abroad was an unexpected bonus, especially when I was sent to cover a volcanic eruption in Iceland.

I left on a Sunday night on an Icelandair red-eye and met up with my GMA crew in Reykjavík. From there we took a two-hour helicopter ride, flying over a glacier of endless ice and snow. Suddenly the backdrop changed as we reached the volcano. A fissure of a volcano is like a giant artery leading to the heart (known as the *caldera*) of the volcano that pops from below the surface. The fissure can open up as long as a half mile and spew a giant pool of lava.

The lava of this volcano glowed and popped as it flowed up from the earth. Even from the helicopter, we could hear the oozing and crackling. I have seen a lot of miracles of nature, but this one took my breath away. The lava was a deep orange-red, as if the sun was on fire. I wanted to reach down and grab it with my hands just to see if it was real. It was hard to tell from our vantage point just how high the geysers were bubbling, and as the chopper descended, the heat rose dramatically. The power of Mother Earth never disappoints me. It's almost impossible to take your eyes away from what she can conjure up.

We landed a safe distance from the fissure on the glacier where a camp had been set up for the crew. Drones had been positioned for the close-up shots so we would be out of harm's way, but there was a subzero wind chill that could be dangerous if we were exposed to it for too long. The crew and I barely noticed the frigid cold because we were about to make television history. Nobody had ever done a live broadcast of a drone flying into a volcano, and I was part of the team leading the charge.

No one had been able to get this close, gathering temperature and wind data from in and around a lava field like this. The geologist we were interviewing had tears in his eyes, as we revealed the beauty of the lava for millions of viewers. He knew that science had just taken a giant leap forward. The broadcast lasted two hours, and then I flew right back to New York and went straight to the station to do *World News Tonight*. That night, as I drifted off to sleep and thought about this incredible adventure I'd just been on, it almost felt like a dream.

The whirlwind trip spearheading a first-of-its-kind report really should have generated a host of emotions in me. Instead, I just dozed off and went on as usual the next day.

I recently heard a narrator on the Calm meditation app who compared emotions to a fast-moving river. Oftentimes people get swept up in the river, becoming tangled up in their emotions. The woman on the app suggested trying to stand at the edge of the river, feel the water rushing past, and notice all the emotions without allowing them to carry you away. I, the listener, couldn't connect to that example at all. In my reality, I deliberately stay as far away as possible from the river. When things get intense, I choose the helicopter, where the distance gives me a vantage point and keeps me safe. Because to me, emotions are not water . . . they are lava. Emotional lava. Dangerous, untouchable, yet beautiful from afar.

Dr. Wilson refers to this as *dissociation* and most likely I refined my use of it at a young age. The houses I lived in often felt like volcanoes—unpredictable, hot, and dangerous. I wanted to understand what was happening, but only from far away. My default was to get in the helicopter and fly high, away from it. Unfortunately, as I got older, this system created distance in almost all my personal relationships and a deeper divide in identity diffusion.

At the peak of my anorexia in high school, I lied to keep my distance from anybody who threatened my disease. As a young adult, I used casual sex or cheating to create distance from men. Somehow I always found a way to climb back into the helicopter and slam the door shut. If anybody managed to get in, I would push them out, straight into the lava.

I had a pattern of destroying one relationship and quickly getting straight back into a new one. I thought I needed a partner to "complete me." But I've learned that it's nobody's job but mine to complete me, and it's unfair to ask anyone else to do it.

As I was listening to this meditation, I kept thinking, *I don't need to get to the side of the river, I need to come down and drop in once in a while.* And most importantly, I need to see the river of emotion as water and not scalding-hot lava. I need to realize it is okay to touch it once in a while. Not to be washed away in it, because that takes me into another mental issue. But to feel and know that it's okay.

This was a huge breakthrough for me because obviously I was no longer seeing myself up in the helicopter. Dr. Wilson agreed with me and attributed it to the work I've done to finally come into my own. I am on the path to complete myself.

Identifying the way my brain was trained from childhood to make me feel safe was the first step in honoring myself. That awareness allows me to authentically connect not only to myself but to other people. I need to be emotionally stable and wise for my children, and I feel like I'm capable of that now. I need to protect them as much as I can, and to share with them the tools I have accumulated in my belt in my nearly forty years.

And I will warn them it isn't always easy. The river of our emotions can feel scary and overwhelming even when you're standing on the side watching it go by. But I will also assure them that feelings will pass, and that they are always safe as long as they appreciate the wonder and the truth of who they are.

When you love somebody you worry about them, especially your children. Dr. Wilson refers to this as "healthy attachment." That's an unfamiliar place to be for me, but my kids make it worth it for me to get there. I've learned that feelings are not necessarily good or bad. They just are. I remind myself that it's good to feel. It means I'm alive and I'm okay. I even let my feelings knock me around a little and eventually they move past me.

Three months into the pandemic and the stay-at-home order, the "new normal" for Ben's and my weekends consisted of dedicating every moment to the kids, and when they were napping, we would get in our workouts and focus on us. One recent day, Ben (who is on WPIX 11 in New York weekdays from 9 to 11 a.m.) wanted to shoot a segment while the kids were asleep and he needed me to be the camera operator. He asked if I could work out early—he would take the boys for a drive because it was a gorgeous day and they needed to get out of the house. Both kids love looking at cars and both seem so serene on car rides.

I agreed and was almost excited to have a moment to myself. Hell, before this global pandemic, I traveled so much I had alone time constantly. Too much. I was loving being home with my family and it was changing the way I looked at my life going forward. This would be a good test, I thought.

They left, I went to change into my workout clothes, and as soon as my foot hit the step to go downstairs the worst possible image flooded my brain. I saw our SUV with all my boys (including our new dog, Brando) getting into a car accident. They were all dead in my mind. Such a horrific daydream. I kept shaking my head, telling myself to stop thinking that way. That isn't me. I am not a worrier.

Granted, as soon as I became a parent, I started having these types of extreme nightmares or daydreams, for example when we got the house and I was militant about people going barefoot versus wearing socks while carrying the baby down the stairs, because I feared they would slip—and I kept seeing the image of the baby falling out of our arms.

Those were new feelings for me because I had never cared so much about anything in my life, and I am not an anxious person. Dr. Wilson explained that it was the transition of moving, having a new baby, Ben's new job out of state, and all these anxieties coming together. I was actually feeling and that was good.

But when those fears cropped up, I would tamp them down and move on. I never cried or got overwhelmed by these moments.

But on this day, when that foot hit the stair and my mind went to that dark and horrible scenario, the nightmare kept playing. I felt the fear briefly froze me, and I had to crouch on the ground. I grabbed my chest. My chest was tight. My breathing labored. Tears started flowing uncontrollably, and I audibly yelled, "NOOOOOO."

As if the accident were really happening. I then said out loud in the empty house:

"Stop. Stop. Stop."

Yes, I sounded like Betty in the Shangri-Las song, "Leader of the Pack." Instead of yelling to Johnny, I mean, Ben, I was telling myself to stop, my brain to stop. Just stop this—over and over. For the next twenty minutes I just went back and forth trying to activate the Elsa button but without success. Emotion was winning. I got on the treadmill, tears and all, thinking that my body could tell my mind to shut down. I worked hard to convince myself that calling or texting Ben was a bad idea that in itself could cause an accident and cause me to lose my whole family in one second.

I even went so far as to think about who would come

to console me after this terrible thing happened. And that I would do the same for these people. Even during the pandemic. My brain was like a never-ending fire whirl spitting debris and horrible thoughts. And my body could not stop it. I got on the mat to do the abs section of my workout and tears just kept rolling. It was amazing. And then I let go. I let myself feel, I stopped fighting, I cried, and as soon as it was all out, I started feeling better.

Granted, full release happened when I heard my kids' little feet on the floor above me when they got home. But what a lesson for my inner Elsa. I do have feelings. I do cry. I can't and probably shouldn't conceal it all, all the time.

Ben always makes fun of me because he says I didn't cry at our wedding. He was a beautiful mess of tears and ugly cry faces. I did cry, but I was using all my *Frozen* power that day and shed tears . . . gracefully and in a controlled manner.

Of course, the feelings I had on the stairs and in our home gym were so much about the lack of control we all feel right now in this pandemic. The uncertainty would make even the strongest concealer break down. And it has. But I am taking this as a moment for reflection and growth. Trying to create a new template of what I am allowed to do even when I am not alone. I am allowed to feel. To cry. To scream in frustration. Emoting is okay up to a certain level.

Here's my plan now. Whenever I feel myself detaching, opening the door to go up in my helicopter, I let myself fly up a bit, but not too high. I lower myself to the side of the river. I prepare myself with a life jacket and anchor myself to the side. I dip my toes in the water, even when the river has whitecaps and moves faster than I want it to. I look for the beauty in the river, but I don't put myself in danger. I don't let it take me.

And for you reading this—that's something to think about. Are you a person who gets easily caught up in the river of emotion, or are you more likely to take refuge in the helicopter? Maybe you let it rush you away every time by jumping in. I encourage you to take a moment and think about where you are in relation to the river of emotions, and how you might be able to find your place on the side, enjoying all that it, and life, have to offer.

Back to that sunny day in Chicago. I decided to walk the winding journey because it was midafternoon and I felt safe enough. I also knew that as soon as I felt fear, I could push it down. So I started the walk, extra-vigilant and confident when I approached the underground passage. I was about a hundred yards away and changing the song on my iPod when I glanced up and saw a bicyclist on the path coming toward me. I looked down briefly again and hit pause just in time to look up and see this person barely miss me at high speed and veer off into the grass on the side of the path. I first thought he was having a stroke or something. Why else would he come right at me? But as he got up, he chucked his bicycle at me. It fell short. Then this man in his tight spandex shorts, matching top with a race number (when he clearly was not in a race), and helmet started charging at me.

This was not the foe I had imagined in my head. Mine had been more of a homeless, drunk, or high person who was delusional and frightening. Like the one I had run into under the other bridge in Chicago (recounted in *Natural Disaster*).

More than a year earlier, when I was about to move to Chicago, my mom, who was terrified of the big city and her baby living in it, bought me some Mace. I hadn't ever used it but always knew where it was in my purse. So, almost out of instinct, I realized my hand was already in my purse when the biker had tossed the bike. As soon as he charged, I pulled the Mace out of the bag as he yelled at me "for being on the wrong side of the path, what are you trying to do fucking kill people? Fuck you. Fuck you!" (I wasn't on the wrong side, by the way. His imaginary race must not have been going well.)

Whatever the case, I whipped out that Mace and pointed it right at him. He immediately stopped in his tracks, and although it made absolutely no sense, I planted my feet in almost superhero stance and said, "Oh yeah?"

Then proceeded to spray the Mace just to the side of him. It came out in a sad arched stream—with much less fervor than I had imagined it would. Probably because it was expired.

It all happened so fast I didn't even have a chance to feel

the emotion of fear or anger or whatever this guy's tight shorts had made him feel.

But my comical defense was enough to make him grab his bike and ride off, murmuring, "Fucking Mace, pepper spray, fuck you. . . ."

I was still in shock as I watched him ride away. I slowly released my outstretched arm and stared at the spray.

In this case, all the emotion could be cured by humor. 'Cause that was fucking funny.

I started giggling as I put the spray back in my purse.

CHAPTER FOURTEEN
CAT-5 RISK ASSESSMENT

A s I noted earlier, FEARLESS GINGER always remains calm in the face of physical danger. But these days, the one thing that does scare me is that I won't be able to grow into my feelings and allow myself to feel and fear. If I could capture that healthy balance, it would make me truly FEARLESS GINGER.

When I returned from covering Hurricane Michael, the Category-5 hurricane that swallowed Mexico Beach, Florida, and shredded Panama City, I was confused. Everyone, from my husband to my bosses, was angry with me.

I've been in many hurricanes, from Katrina to Sandy, tropical storms aplenty. There have been moments of awe but never fear when I storm-chase. I always act conservatively in my choices and never want to be a part of the problem or need to be rescued. That said, I do push the limits a bit.

When Hurricane Michael quickly went from tropical

storm to buzz-saw behemoth potential, I knew I had to be there. I flew down the day before the storm and landed in Tallahassee at about 3 p.m. The forecast cone of uncertainty was tight; we knew Michael would come onshore the next morning somewhere south of Panama City.

Tallahassee was the only airport with available flights to get me from New York after *GMA* and before *World News Tonight*. When you have to make connections, it is always a roll of the dice that you will make that second show of the day, but this time I did. When we safely landed in the Florida panhandle, field producer Brandon Chase picked me up with Los Angeles–based field producer Jenna Harrison. This was a Cat-5 hurricane dream team. As I detailed in my first book, the "field producer" relationship is one of the most important in my job. We drop into highly stressful situations and you need to have partners who you enjoy being around, since many of these trips get long and require endless days and nights without much sleep. Jenna and Brandon are both producers I had worked with and adored, so I had a good feeling. Jenna grew up in Georgia and had never seen a tornado. I got to provide commentary during her first one on our first assignment together. Brandon and I had worked together extensively on meteorological events from tornadoes to floods to fires over the years, and he was always one of my favorites to be on the road with. Both he and Jenna are the type of producers who not only make sure we have what we need and that we get on the air, but they actually help produce stories.

They picked me up, and we gassed up and got extra fuel for generators, strapping the cans to the top of the Pathfinder we had rented. As we traveled south on 319 toward our target site for the storm, Apalachicola, the bungees were clanging against the top and sides of the vehicle. We laughed as we tried to get to the *World News* live shot on time.

When we arrived, I jumped out of the SUV and we quickly did a night-before-the-storm forecast from the center of low-lying Apalachicola. Right before the live shot, we spotted an alligator in the bay popping its head up, seemingly in an effort to get on TV.

When I started my broadcast that night, the mood changed. The warnings were dire. From where we stood to Panama City Beach, up to twelve feet of storm surge was possible with winds in excess of 150 mph. This was going to be bad. Storm surge is the number one killer in hurricanes. It is the unavoidable swell in water that powerfully strips towns on the coast. The power of the surge, of that barrage of ocean water, is more ruthless than anyone understands. I had seen the damage before, I had heard the stories, but I had never seen a surge of that height with my own eyes.

After *World News Tonight* wrapped, we drove to the Best Western in Apalachicola, which had been booked by the assignment desk in New York for us and the crew. As soon as we pulled in, Brandon hopped out to get all the keys, and I got out of the car to look around the grounds of the hotel. Having weathered hurricanes of different strengths, I'd created a checklist I like to go through for safety and then pair it with making great TV. This Best Western was not hitting any of the checklist points, and when Brandon came back out, it got worse.

"I think we have a problem. Only one room on the second floor. The rest are on the ground level," he told us.

Apalachicola is a fishing town with a bay and very little protection from the ocean. Brandon is not a meteorologist, but he had worked with us enough to know that we needed to be on the second floor for storm surge and flooding concerns. I looked around the building, surrounded by trees that could act like projectiles in 100-plus-mph winds. I looked at Brandon and said, "We can't stay here. I am not dying at a Best Western in Apalachicola. That's just not how I go. Let's head west and see what we can find."

When these storms happen, most TV networks are in place and hotels are often booked almost a week in advance.

We started up Highway 98 west to Port St. Joe, and the sun was already starting to set. I quickly prayed that somewhere in this town there would be some second-floor rooms available. Many places were already boarded up; others were at capacity. The Weather Channel had taken a lot of the rooms.

I knew that by going one more town west, we put our-selves much closer to the most dangerous part of the storm, but I was just so turned off by the idea of Apalachicola's Best Western by then that I was willing to stay up late to try to find the "unicorn" of shelter. I begged Brandon and Jenna to press on, and they were with me.

When we arrived in Mexico Beach after 8:30 p.m., it was difficult to see the charm of this old beach town. It truly exemplifies the old guard of the Florida panhandle. Pristine beaches and businesses that were established some seventy-plus years ago. It is a place where generations of families have spent their summers and school breaks enjoying the usually serene Gulf of Mexico.

The streets were dead, most places boarded up, and there really weren't any commercial hotels. We got to the end of the mile-long town and decided to turn back. Then Brandon saw someone boarding up what looked like a condo complex. The man told us he could call the manager of the building and see if she might know of a place we could stay.

Again, we weren't hotel-less; I just had a feeling that we needed to be here. In Mexico Beach. I knew the surge would be the worst here. I also knew that these newer buildings were built to code and would offer us both the safety we needed and spectacular visuals as the storm made landfall the next day. Our forecasts had been accurate so far, and at fifteen hours out, this was not a storm that would surprise anyone.

We drove back east to the other condo building, called the Summerhouse, to meet Kimberly Kennedy, the manager of both buildings. When she hopped out of her SUV, all I saw was a petite Southern angel. Kimberly, a tiny blond in flip-flops, cutoff shorts, and a tank top, had two phones and was masterfully managing several buildings and calls simultaneously. Everyone who owned the condos was understandably worried about their property, but very few people had stayed behind. Kimberly lived down the road and had promised the owners of the condos that she would care for their properties.

She made a few quick phone calls and came back with great news: We could stay in the Summerhouse.

Kimberly showed us to our rooms on the third and fifth floors. Behind the modern and obviously recently updated decor were cement walls, cement ceilings, and under us, cement pylons that went deep into the earth.

I asked more questions about the building code, how and when the building was built, and I felt confident that this was our spot, not just for tonight but for the hurricane itself. Hurricane-proof windows and doors, deep moorings for those pylons that held the building above street level. They had seen strong storms before in the panhandle, but it had been at least fifty years since a Category 5 had hit anywhere close.

We settled in for the night, got up to do GMA with a writhing Gulf of Mexico behind us, and started seeing the water creep onto the beach by 9 a.m.

The surge was going to be at least twelve feet, and now I could feel the energy of the storm. My fearless skill in risk aversion from years of chasing settled in. I'd seen the eye in Sandy, had temporarily lived in the destruction of Katrina, and weathered several lesser hurricanes and tropical storms since then, including the devastating Florence just a few weeks earlier in Wilmington, North Carolina. But this was not a slow rainmaker like Harvey or Florence. This was a Cat 5 that would slice through the coast fast. I felt confident staying, but was I being reckless? I called Travis Herzog, a trusted friend and chief meteorologist at our ABC affiliate in Houston, who knows tropical weather. He said I had guts, but he agreed, we would be okay. I checked in with our weekend meteorologist, Rob Marciano, who was in Panama City Beach, which would be on the left side or weaker side of the storm. He said it was going to be wild, but he agreed that we would be okay.

We told the satellite truck to leave because of the potential for surge. And then we went up to wait it out.

We did our live shots for the special report starting at 11 a.m.

George Stephanopoulos was anchoring and the conditions deteriorated quickly as the storm was moving 10 to 15 mph due north toward us. I stood on the balcony, showing the winds picking up; with each live hit on TV the winds became angrier. Once we started to see debris fly (usually after sustained winds of 60 mph), it was too dangerous to stay on the balcony, so we brought the setup inside. Every tropical storm and hurricane I have been in has a sound like a car wash or a washing machine, but the sound that Michael started making was not something I had heard, seen, or felt—ever.

Michael was a Cat 4 (Cat 5 when they went back to solidify observations), and in any storm, the outer bands can be dangerous with flash flooding, tornadoes, and wind, but the eye wall is where the widespread, deadly damage happens. We were going to be directly in the eye wall. Not just in the eye wall but in the northeast quadrant of the eye wall, the part we call the dirty side of the storm. It's dirty because the worst of the surge, winds, and tornadoes is always found in that northeast quadrant. It's where the forward motion of the storm combines with the speed of the winds in the hurricane itself, magnifying the intensity.

Our broadcasting equipment was holding on through these winds, and I was so happy we could keep giving the information and showing the images of the start of the eye wall. As winds ticked up closer to 90 mph, more debris started flying and some scaffolding slid down the street. When I looked down to check my radar once more, it wouldn't refresh, and that was the telltale sign. Shit would now be hitting the actual fan because cell service was weakening. My mind flooded with the first fear I would have that day: losing access to data, communication, and information.

"Um, Ginger—the ocean is in the street," Brandon said.

I looked through the sliding glass door, and sure enough, in the minute I had looked down at my radar, the water had crept over the dunes and the first block of houses and was crossing Highway 98 at a rapid pace, coming toward our building.

By this point I had made a mental note of the homes that composed that first line of defense right on the oceanfront. They were still standing. But water is powerful. I knew they did not have a great shot at withstanding what was about to bubble up.

I rounded the corner to the bedroom slider, and in the seven seconds it took me to walk between rooms, the storm surge had grown to at least ten feet. It was now lapping at the second floor below us. I never use the word *surprise* in forecasting because I am rarely surprised. At that moment I was not just surprised; I was stunned at how quickly the bubble of storm surge had overwhelmed the coast.

I squinted my eyes to see through the whipping sheets of rain in order to gauge how high the surge was climbing. Highway 98 was now the ocean, and in it I saw something that made my head tilt like a dog when it hears a noise that it cannot identify. My eyes strained even more to focus on the debris in the middle of Highway 98. I cupped my mouth and gasped loudly as I realized that that was not just debris, but rather an entire roof, still connected to the blue house that we had been reporting in front of the whole day. That blue house was now bobbing down the highway, surrounded by the ocean.

I was in awe.

My mind jumped to five years earlier when I stood with Patricia Dresch, a woman in Staten Island who had survived Superstorm Sandy.

As the surreal visuals played out in front of me here in Florida, I could hear Patricia's New York accent, her voice clearly recounting her petrifying story. She explained how the water started coming into her home within a minute of the ocean reaching her street—rushing in the front door and back door at the same time, moments after the family had finished dinner. She and her husband and daughter ran up the stairs thinking that would buy them some time. It only bought them sixty seconds. From the second floor they saw the sliding glass door on the second floor give way, water pouring through the busted windows, and then Patricia described the most surreal phenomenon: their home was twisted off its foundation. The water started pulling the house apart, walls fell away, and the waves battered the family as they tried to stay above water. She held her daughter, arms locked, until a large piece of debris, maybe even a wall, hit them in the head. Patricia fought to get to the surface of the water and called for her daughter, exposed in the roiling surge, but couldn't find her. She heard her husband calling her for help; she grasped at power lines to stay afloat but could not fight the pervasive surge. She remembers "landing" on a pile of debris and praying. Five hours later she "woke up" to paramedics standing over her, covering her with a blanket. She was hypothermic but had survived thanks to a rogue flashlight that had ended up in her particular pile of debris. Her husband and daughter had not survived.

Prior to Patricia, no one had ever described storm surge so vividly to me, and when I left that interview, I had an overwhelming feeling that I needed people not just to hear that story, but I needed to help them visualize it. And no, not for the sensational news angle, but for the scientific explanation. When I show a colored line on a coastline to describe ten to fifteen feet of storm surge, people honestly have no idea what it means or what the surge would look like in the moment. To be sure, folks take warnings seriously. I went back and wrote a script for a 3-D graphic hoping ABC would help me create it. They agreed, and for six months we worked so hard on these unbelievable graphics that show the strength and reality of storm surge. It is a vibrant, albeit scary, visualization of what that surge would feel like in a person's home. We shot it with me on a green screen, describing the home twisting off its foundation and bobbing into the water.

And now I was watching that graphic, and Patricia's chilling story, come to life right in front of me.

I kept thinking, *I am watching people die.* A wash of helplessness came over me. I knew my colleagues and I were safe in this building, but who was in that house I just watched twirl down the street? This ocean was not going to let up for at least forty-five minutes, based on the last radar image I saw. My obsession with watching the debris in the storm surge was brought back to reality when I heard a gasp.

Jenna was backed up against the wall behind me, hands cupped over her mouth in awe of the storm. "Are we okay? Ginger, are we going to be okay?" she asked.

Jenna didn't have her glasses and couldn't see the water level and it appeared much higher to her than it was. Jenna's, I may point out, was a normal reaction to being in a Category-5 hurricane.

I assured her we were okay.

Meanwhile, quietly, in my brain, I was aware that this was the first time I even considered that we might not be okay. I kept running the numbers. The surge wouldn't go above fifteen feet. And we were thirty or so feet up. We were safe. I had made sure we didn't stay on the top floor just in case a gust of 150 mph or greater had a shot at ripping the roof off. But in this building, all the walls were made of cement. And it wasn't even shaking. I knew we were okay.

Stoic doesn't begin to describe my photographer, Jay Schexnyder, and Tim Wall, our audio guy. Brandon's quiet demeanor was pretty unique, too. It was eerily quiet as we all just stared and watched that quaint little town that had gone untouched for more than half a century get erased by Hurricane Michael.

"Coming to you, Ginger." George Stephanopoulos prepared to toss to me. We all started to look alive, and I dove straight in.

"George, I have never seen anything like this in my life. I just watched a well-built home ripped from its foundation and roll down the street."

My voice cracked and many viewers and my bosses would later tell me that they could hear the fear in my voice. That fear was not for us, though; it was for the people I knew were dying around us.

When the control room tried to come back to us again, we had no signal and wouldn't be able to communicate for another twenty-four hours.

At that point we just sat and watched. Most of the time in storm coverage you never stop running, producing content. But this moment was different, not only because we couldn't be live, but because the storm felt so powerful that none of us could really move. It wasn't safe or interesting because the camera couldn't really capture what was happening outside, so in this unique moment in all of our careers, we got to watch it play out—and not through a lens. It was probably one of the most "in the moment" moments I have had in my career and life.

After thirty minutes of playing pure spectator to the raw power of our atmosphere, we witnessed the mesmerizing car-wash effect play out like a commercial-free episode of *Planet Earth*; all we were missing was David Attenborough's voice. I mindlessly snacked on white chocolate trail mix and consumed far more than I would have normally. Calories don't count in hurricanes. Especially in a Cat 5. As the trail mix ran out, Mother Nature's prime-time show without the screen came to a close. The surge quickly receded and the winds relaxed.

When the winds dropped below 60 mph, we were able to go upstairs to the other rooms; they were all soaked from the sideways rain but not a window or door was broken in our building. This place was a fortress.

Unfortunately that was not the case for most of Mexico Beach. The beautiful surf town was nearly wiped clean; Highway 98 was covered in sand after the ocean had left its footprint. By sunset, the winds were well below 30 mph, so I felt safe enough to venture out while we still had some natural light. We didn't wander too far because power lines and dangerous debris littered the streets as far as the eye could see.

It was bizarrely silent. No sirens, no search and rescue. It had been six hours since the peak of the storm, and it looked like a movie set for a disaster film that had wrapped for the day.

We met up with Kimberly and the two other couples who had survived the storm in our same building. We did interviews backlit with the purple hue of the sunset settling over the wreckage behind the interviewees. The tears were flowing as these folks went through the same shock I see in every survivor of every natural disaster. Fire, flood, tornado, hurricane—our mental-health response is as predictable as the storms themselves.

We went to bed after trying feverishly to get the satellite phone to work. I had managed to get out one tweet saying we were fine, so the station used that in their broadcasts. But that final tiny bar next to the AT&T symbol on my phone blinked away by 7 p.m. and we were all alone.

At about 10 p.m. we decided there was very little we could do except wait for the light of day, so we went to bed. As I fell asleep, a bout of sleep paralysis hit. I saw Patricia on her pile of debris praying and crying for her daughter and husband, shivering and near death (her body temperature was eighty-four when paramedics found her). When I was able to move, I opened the sliding glass door hoping I might be able to hear someone calling for help. Nothing.

Riding the slide of postadrenaline from that nightmare

and the day itself, I slipped back into deep sleep. I was rocked awake from that slumber a few hours later when I heard screams outside my door.

As my eyes struggled to open, I noticed that the room had turned hot and the smell was already dank from that inch or two of water that had poured in during the height of Michael.

I stepped out of the bed and felt the smush of the rug, sopping wet still, squeezed between my toes. I carefully navigated the wet tile to open the slider. The sea of debris hadn't been altered, but now there were two men waving flashlights yelling, "ABC! Ginger Zee!"

I called down in response and waved my arms to show them I was up on a fifth-floor balcony. Then my reflex was to clutch my boobs since I didn't have a bra on, as if the men were going to be able to see my nipples. As if that mattered at this very moment.

"Are you Ginger from ABC News?"

"Yes," I said from the balcony.

"We are here to get you out."

I asked them to come up so we didn't have to yell, and I went to get Brandon.

When the guys met us in the exposed corridor, we learned that they were not the National Guard, not police nor fire. They were volunteers from the next town over: Christian Oakes and Jason Maddy (now formally known as Disaster

Task Force US). They said they could helicopter us out. We refused the offer. They needed to get other people out. There were injured people, I was sure. And I still hadn't seen or heard about any formal rescue operations.

They told us about the missions they had already completed as volunteers, including evacuating an oxygen-dependent eighty-one-year-old woman and her daughter, plus another two dozen rescues.

We told them we were fine and had plenty of supplies. They left us Gatorade and granola bars anyway.

The next morning, I awoke to the sound of construction. I was hopeful that official help had arrived.

When we emerged from the building, the road was littered with roofs, vehicles, and tons of sand and debris. No one would be able to drive out. No one had a car. The surge had taken our rented Pathfinder with its dings on the roof and we couldn't even find it. It had been washed into the retention pond behind the building and sank. Christian and Jason pulled it out a few months later and sent us a picture.

Jay's car was upside down in the parking lot, waterlogged, and very little inside was salvageable.

The only way to get out of town was to hike. We packed up all our stuff and started dragging our suitcases through the sand-filled streets, snaking around the dangerous debris and power lines.

We talked to people along the way, the sun baking us already. The construction noise was coming from a backhoe operated by a guy who had hot-wired it in order to help his town. He was a local—still no authorities. The damage just kept getting more horrific with every block. I snapped photos with street signs knowing that I could share them later—I had seen in Katrina and Sandy how much these images helped when I shared them with folks who couldn't get in to check on their loved ones or their homes.

We learned that many people who had stayed hadn't wanted to, but, unlike in any storm I had covered in the past, had had no way out. No cars, no friends or family, no one to take them to a shelter. It was devastating to hear these stories. One couple we met told us that when the surge made it inland five blocks to their mobile home, they knew they wouldn't survive inside, so they put on life jackets and held their two dogs as the water engulfed them. They found a boat and climbed inside, riding out the worst of the storm for more than two hours. The woman, Talia Butcher, gave me her mother's phone number. She wanted me to call her as soon as our satellite phone worked or we got to cell service so she would know that her daughter and son-in-law had survived.

We hiked two miles to the bridge that separates the end of Mexico Beach from the forested area by the Tyndall Air Force Base to meet up with Todd McKee, a freelance field producer who was on his way to extract us.

We waited for hours in the sun with the flies and the smell of broken construction from the 1950s (an interesting and memorable scent I had become accustomed to when renovating my home in Flint, which was built in 1959).

During that time, other media showed up. Then FEMA, the Coast Guard . . . everyone arrived. It had been eighteen hours since the storm. It had been at least ten hours since it was safe to be out and saving lives. But this was the first official help we had seen. I have come to understand that in disasters, with all the red tape, the planning or lack thereof, the bottom line is it's the communication. I was too tired to press that story at that moment.

I focused my energy on telling the stories of the people we had met.

We had finally gotten the satellite phone to work, so I started dialing families of survivors we had met during our two-mile hike that morning.

I am not sure there is a better feeling in a post-storm situation than calling a mother and telling her that her daughter survived. That is what I got to do for Talia's mother.

She gasped and screamed with joy when she learned that her daughter and son-in-law had survived. I called at least five other families to pass along the good news. Tears were flowing each time I heard them profusely thank me.

Todd finally showed up. It had taken him two hours to drive thirty miles because of all the fallen trees. As we drove away, I turned once more to stare at the western edge of Mexico Beach and a pang of guilt hit. I always hate leaving a storm zone and always feel intense guilt. But I knew we had to go tell these stories and couldn't do it from there.

As we entered Panama City, you could quickly tell it was not much better off than Mexico Beach. It appeared there was damage to every single building. Trees and extreme wind damage had shredded the town, which looked very much like a war-torn city. We got to a hotel that was less damaged than some of the others so we could try to rest before *World News Tonight*. The rooms were hot without electricity and the smell of destruction was overwhelming, laced with the smell of gas, likely from a generator that must have been being used for the kitchen.

I ripped the comforter off the bed in the room hoping the sheets were somewhat clean. Not that I was or would be clean myself for a few days. I had done this drill before. During Katrina I didn't even have the hotel bed. I had slept in a van, so this was luxury. I had started to drift off when . . . *Rrrrrriiiiiinnnnnnggggg!*

The fire alarms began blaring. I gathered my things and followed the evacuation route groggily. The fumes had set off the fire alarm. They were too strong and the management needed us to evacuate the building.

Instead of waiting, Brandon and I decided to try to nap

in the car closer to where we would be doing our live shot for *World News Tonight.* This would be unlike my typical stories post-storm. David Muir wanted me to start the broadcast with him.

David and I had worked together for seven years by this point. I had started on the weekends with him. He made me such a staple of his show because we just work together. And here we were in the damage from the strongest hurricane in most of our lifetimes (since Andrew in 1992), bringing the story to America. David had had quite the adventure himself in Panama City, I learned. As he was broadcasting after I went off the air, the awning he was broadcasting under collapsed on his rental car.

Dear National Rental Car, So sorry. Love, Ginger and David.

The story we told that night was harrowing; the journey for the people who lived there would be years long.

That next morning, I did one more hit for GMA and then made my way back to New York. On the way, I was trying to manage my guilt about leaving. I got to go home to my electricity, my mailbox, my comforts. The people down here had lost all of those things and nearly sixty people lost their lives.

When I got home, I was elated to see Ben and the kids, but I could tell Ben was upset. He does not have a great poker face and usually expresses himself with full transparency. We had a nice dinner with the kids and got them down for bed, then I went to take a bath, and I said, "Please tell me what's wrong."

He explained that the day of the storm he kept getting texts from family and friends saying, *What is she thinking? You have children. Why is she doing this?*

He was in the middle of taping his shows in Nashville (he was cohosting a show with Kelly Pickler called *Pickler & Ben* at the time), so he didn't watch (he doesn't like to when I am in a storm, even if he is home) and rarely follows my storm-chasing or other adventures because he is unnerved by pretty much everything I do. Ben has a low tolerance for risk, likes control, and finds joy in less dangerous endeavors.

He and I had a deep talk that night, and he expressed his anger with my choices. Why would I do what I'd done and chance the kids losing me? Why do that for a job? So I could look good? So I could get more airtime?

I was shocked. I still didn't feel like I had taken a risk that was that bad. But when I asked myself the other questions, I think the issue had grown well beyond my deep curiosity for meteorology. Of course, I knew I was going to make good TV. That was part of why I had left Apalachicola in the first place.

When I went to my next therapy session, I dove into this with Dr. Wilson.

He told me that I had developed a very high tolerance for risk. That I have had both the experience and the education to play the stats, but I'd also had luck. Some of it is luck. And I don't see that because every time I "get away with it without a scratch," it builds a risk tolerance that surpasses a healthy level. That is not "normal."

Nothing new there. I had never really been normal with risk or with fear.

I went to Ben and promised I would never take another chance like that. As I'm writing, I just came back from covering Hurricane Laura. Since I'd left for the Gulf Coast less than two years after Michael, a lot had changed. We are in a global pandemic, and even getting on an airplane presents far more risk than it did six months ago. I knew that Laura would be bad, so I knew it was my responsibility to be there to bring attention so folks knew the gravity of the storm and could evacuate the areas that needed to be evacuated. As I was packing, Ben started acting strangely. I asked him what was wrong, and he said he was scared. He was scared that I would make a "bad choice" again.

I assured him, even back then, that it was not a bad choice, but perhaps it was a little too high on the risk assessment for our family. After spending six months at home with Ben, Adrian, and Miles, I'm feeling more attached to them than ever.

I made my target this time Port Arthur, Texas. I knew we would not get the storm surge there and I pushed to be on the waterfront. Michael Kreisel, the assignment desk editor, along with Wendy Fisher, who had sat me down post-Michael to tell me I was not allowed to ever do that again, must have been on the same wavelength as Ben. Because she didn't trust me. She and Ben said I was not allowed to stay on the water even if the building looked okay.

Turns out the only condo we could get on the water did not have the same specs as the Summerhouse in Mexico Beach. It was a far riskier choice *if* the storm moved west at all. Along the current track, that dirty side of the storm was going to hit Louisiana, just to our east. I knew we would be on the windy, but relatively safer side of the eye wall and that's why I felt confident. But no one believed me.

Sure enough, we barely got a 75-mph gust, while the town I really wanted to be in, Cameron, was where Hurricane Laura made landfall as a Category 4. It was cut off for days by the water and collapsed from the winds.

In all honesty, there is a big part of me that pined for the images my colleagues were seeing in Lake Charles just north of Cameron, where the casinos were peppered with debris and windows were blown out by nearly 140-mph winds. The morning after Laura made landfall, on two hours of sleep, I dedicated myself to getting to Cameron. That would be my contribution to this storm. But the roads were covered in downed power lines and we had to turn around. As soon as I knew that the story couldn't be told, and I knew Matt Gutman and Rob Marciano and Victor Oquendo and the teams that were on the ground would be more than enough to cover the aftermath, I told the desk I was ready to go home. I was going to have to isolate and not see my family until I got a negative coronavirus test anyway, so this plan would put me back with my boys sooner.

And that moment right there, that was when I knew I had changed. The two years since Michael had changed my risk assessment. I allowed the disappointment to roll over me. I wrote in my journal to express how that had made me feel, but when I walked back in the door and was able to proudly tell Ben that I had done my job all while getting lower wind gusts than we had had in tropical storm Isaias a few weeks before in our own backyard in New York, I felt like I started to regain his trust. I felt like he saw that I respected our family and my own life.

My Cat-5 risk assessment was down to a Cat 4. I don't think this means I will never find myself in a Mexico Beach situation again, but I will have these healthier emotional attachments. I will think of others before myself and what it would mean if my luck ran out.

CHAPTER FIFTEEN
THE MASK

I started writing this chapter well before we all had to get used to wearing masks because of Covid-19. The "mask" I am referring to in this chapter is not the coronavirus-prevention mask that became so oddly political, but rather the mask of our facial expressions (often smiling when we're not at all content) that we all wear at times to cover how we truly feel.

On August 31, 2020, I saw a Facebook post from our female meteorologist group:

TEXAS FORECASTER, "A SMILE AS BIG AS TEXAS" SUDDENLY DIES was the headline.

Another broadcast meteorologist had died by suicide. I say another because we have lost several in the last few years. I can't say with confidence that there is a propensity for folks in broadcast meteorology to take their own lives due to hours, PTSD from storms, or just overall rejection and lack of self-worth in this business. I can't say that with stats, but there does seem to be an anecdotal correlation.

Under the image of Kelly Plasker, a morning meteorologist at the NBC affiliate in Lubbock, Texas, the messages with heart emojis and prayer hands filled the comments section. They spoke of the profound loss she had experienced when her teenage son had died by suicide just two years before. How she had bravely suffered through it all with a smile.

And so many of the comments said:

You would never know that under that brilliant smile there was such pain.

Those comments made me angry.

Really? At this point in our world, we don't know that people who are suffering use a smile to cover their pain? C'mon.

I think we should all learn from these clichés and realize that that smile, that broad, unwavering smile, is often the calling card that something *is* wrong. I know it always was for me. The obsession with happiness or the expectation that happiness must rule our lives is a major problem.

I love leafing through my oma's photos from the Netherlands. The square black-and-white photos feature my grandmother in her late twenties right after World War II, gorgeous and natural, far from skinny, and unquestionably confident. She and the people around her were not posing with fake smiles. Even at the beach, with their arms around each other in the late 1940s and early 1950s, they are at best, "smizing."

In my most Carrie Bradshaw moment of this book, I couldn't help but wonder, when did the smile become the default expression? When did we societally start having to smile in photos? When did we have to smile when we didn't feel like it?

In my quick research, there seems to be some explanation for the smile as a default in photographs starting with tech-nological advancements in the late 1800s (the photo could be taken faster, so holding a smile wasn't as tedious). A *Time* magazine article theorized that in the early days of photogra-phy, people didn't smile because they were trying to re-create a painted portrait in which subjects rarely smiled.

In fact, a big smile in a photo or painting during that period was an indication that the subject might be mentally unstable, drunk, or simply a clown.

Isn't that fascinating? At the time, a smile was interpreted as a potential problem. And now, when we see a photo of someone who isn't smiling, we assume something must be wrong.

When did a smile go from psychologically off to main-stream? It seems this may have been an American-made phe-nomenon thanks to a post-WWII 1950s Kodak advertising campaign featuring cameras, film, and lots of photos of people sporting wide smiles.

Photography quickly became part of happy times and special occasions, so the smile evolved as an expected element. In the *Time* article, a study of yearbook photos clearly shows this evolution of style in portrait photos from serious expressions to smiling faces.

These days, when we're all photographers and can take high-quality images with our phones at no expense, a perfect smile isn't quite as important. My favorite shots remind me of Oma's images from years ago!

In a hilarious 2016 *Vox* article, "America Is Obsessed with Happiness—and It's Making Us Miserable," British author Ruth Whippman writes after moving to America:

> It seems as though happiness in America has become the overachiever's ultimate trophy. A modern trump card, it outranks professional achievement and social success, family, friendship, and even love. Its invocation deftly minimizes others' achievements ("Well, I suppose she has the perfect job and a gorgeous husband, but is she really happy?") and takes the shine off our own.

> It all feels a long way from the British approach I was brought up with. Jefferson knew what he was doing when he wrote that "pursuit of happiness" line, a perfectly delivered slap in the face to his joy-shunning oppressors across the pond. Emotionally awkward and primed for skepticism, the British are generally

uncomfortable around the subject and, as a rule, don't subscribe to the happy ever after. It's not that we don't want to be happy. It just feels embarrassing to discuss it and demeaning to chase it, like calling someone moments after a first date to ask if they like you.

She goes on to describe, with science behind her, that our commitment to happiness actually provokes anxiety.

It's not surprising to me.

We all wear a smile, but that's not most people's default expression. Some of us have perfected the art of not emoting what we truly feel. I think this mask is one of the widely accepted reasons that mental-health problems have attracted such a stigma, and the subject of mental health itself has taken so long to get the attention it deserves. And perhaps, as Whippman found, has itself contributed to some mental-health issues.

My smile and I have a long history. I was a competitive cheerleader in high school, and smiling was one of the most crucial parts of the uniform. In my case, it meshed perfectly with my anorexia and depression. Even if we were injured or slapped in the face at cheer practice, running up and down the stairs in a heat index of one hundred, we were instructed to smile. Even after one of the girls threw up, she was told to get back out there and smile through her nausea.

That's what life feels like to me sometimes—running with

a smile on my face, crying and throwing up at the same time. And to some extent that's okay. I think it's important to be a positive force in the world, but not to the point where I'm hiding myself behind the mask.

And there were too many times when that smile got bigger as I got sadder. I didn't feel comfortable talking to other people and never wanted to share the madness I felt inside. The stigma of mental illness had a lot to do with that. To be vulnerable and share my imperfections was an impossibility while I was in my twenties. The last thing I would ever do was tell people I had attempted suicide or that I was raped or that I had an abortion. If I smiled, they might never even suspect it.

In the early 2000s, had I been transparent with any of that, I think it would have had negative professional implications. Psychotropic medication was not as accepted then as it is today. If you think about it, we are *just now* to the point where people can say "I have depression or anxiety" without radical reactions. Therapy and the use of medication have become more widespread and accepted.

The moment I mention my hospitalization, though, people's ears perk up and their eyes widen—the action I took still has a stigma. And that's what needs to change. Like drug and alcohol rehabilitation, mental rehabilitation should be looked at through the same lens. Disease. Treatment. Thriving.

A 2017 study estimates that one out of five Americans suffers from mental illness. That's more than 46 million people. There are more than two hundred classified forms of mental illness and seven major categories including anxiety disorders, mood disorders, personality disorders, trauma-related disorders, substance-abuse disorders, schizophrenia and psychotic disorders, and eating disorders. Dementia is also sometimes added to that list. It is estimated that more than 20 percent of the homeless population in America suffer from some sort of mental illness.

And yet there are very few of these folks who get long-term treatment.

This has been said in many ways and by many others, but it's important to note. Mental illness is not something you can see, and it's extremely complex when it comes to diagnosis and treatment. For example, many people are never diagnosed (owing mostly to the stigma attached to it). And these people may spend years finding the right treatment or medication that works for them.

There are no blood tests for mental illness. In most cases, it takes a patient being willing and able (and often having the financial means) to do the hard work of internal exploration with the consistent help of a conscientious therapist (sometimes a close friend, counselor, or priest). In my opinion, an official diagnosis can help a person with their internal judgment because it takes the fear that they are suffering alone out of the equation and gives them permission to work through the process of managing their particular mental illness.

But the biggest issue we all must address is that the treatment of mental illness, like other illnesses, needs to focus on preventive medicine: good nutrition, good sleep habits, and physical activity. If those three pillars of health, which are always associated with physical well-being, could be adopted as the first go-to for mental health, we would be able to start with a great foundation for healing.

But we don't do that with mental illness. We need to take it out of the closet so people can get the help they need. Mental illness is pervasive in our society, yet we do not allocate funds or invest in prevention. People who perpetrate mass shootings, veterans suffering with PTSD, first responders with high rates of suicide—all of these things need to be priorities.

It's been nine years since I began therapy with Dr. Wilson and I am stronger than ever. Although I no longer live in constant fear that I could be a danger to myself, I still wake up every day wondering if my depression might ever take me down the rabbit hole again. And it already has in this pandemic, as I described earlier.

The difference this time: I didn't use my mask. I used my team. I used my honesty. And I feel more confident than ever that I will never have to live through that kind of pain again thanks to these tools. For some folks, meditation and therapy

aren't enough and medication can be the key—just like a dia-
betic who has to take insulin every day.

I think I am a person who is hardwired for depression, and
environmental traumas were my triggers. There is a new study
I just read about in *Psychology Today* that contends that anxiety, depression, and PTSD are not disorders at all but rather
our mind and body's responses to adversity.

No matter what they are, they are real. And if we drop
the smile and get comfortable with being okay with how we
feel, being transparent about that to others, then we will be
halfway there. Maybe it's because we're not okay with who
we are.

From an early age we learn from the grown-ups to say, "I
am well, thank you" when asked how we are doing. That is
the common and expected response.

I have to say my mom is the exception to this rule. When
somebody asks her how she's doing, she's honest. "I'm okay but
I've got this knee thing going on." No matter what it is, my
mom will tell you about it. I hated that about her when I was
a kid. Who wants to know your private details? I wanted her
to keep it to herself, like I did. But part of me thinks she was
onto something.

How much healthier and happier might we all be if we
learned to listen a little more, if we cultivated empathy as a
virtue? Because it's not just about being honest when people

ask us how we are doing. When we ask somebody that question, we have to be available to listen to their answer.

Ultimately, like everything in life, it's a balance. Nobody should feel like they have to share everything all the time with everybody. One of life's skills is assessing appropriate situations and evaluating who deserves our trust. What's most important is that we don't let that vulnerability muscle atrophy. Especially these days, when social media and the pandemic have isolated us from each other. We compare ourselves through posts, and too often we feel like we fall short. We forget to take into account that a perfect Instagram post can be somebody else's mask.

So what's the antidote? We have to consciously look for opportunities to authentically connect with each other. Can we make a phone call to a friend even when a text is easier? Can we strive to allow ourselves the imperfections that make us human? Can we go outside of the bubble where everybody shares our opinions?

And can we really embrace a phrase that has become popular lately, "It's okay to not be okay"?

When I was in my twenties, I taught a broadcasting meteorology class at my alma mater, and the number-one rule I gave my students was to smile. Smile no matter what's happening because it makes you seem more appealing, warmer, and accessible. I gave that advice because I believed it. And

I still do. When you're on camera, anything less than a smile will come across as cold and make you less appealing to an audience. Imagine a news anchor or a meteorologist like myself who began their broadcast telling everybody about the bad day they had. Not a great strategy for success. If I could go back to all those students, I would modify this lesson. I would explain that my smile almost killed me, but professionally it has been an indispensable component of my success.

Going forward, I want my smiles to come from within. I'd like to switch from the pursuit of happiness to the pursuit of reality. The candid life, without the mask.

CHAPTER SIXTEEN
JOHN...AGAIN

In my first book, I covered my abusive relationship, but that was the most edited part of my story. When you write a book, you can't just freely say what you want, legally. There was so much more to my story, as there is in any abusive relationship but because of the possible liability, I was not allowed to tell much more for fear that if my abuser thought people could figure out who he was, he could sue me. It was an incredibly upsetting realization. I got a call after the lawyers had gone through the last version of my book and they told me that the bulk of the pages about the abuse had to be taken out. I was with my husband walking in Central Park when I took the call. I hung up and wept. It was a defeated feeling. I felt like John was still controlling me. That feeling eased as I talked to Ben and Dr. Wilson, and eventually I realized my story, even without some of the gory details, was still enough to get the conversation going with other women. They were right. I have been speaking to groups around the country the last two years about mental health and abuse and every stop teaches me something new.

I was doing a speech in Texas and one of the women who spoke said it best. The event was for abused women and a shelter they had created. Her story was unique because she was wealthy. Her emphasis: Abuse does not discriminate. Not based on gender, financial status, or race.

She and her husband lived in a gated community near Dallas—from the outside, life was picture-perfect, but behind that gate, she was in the fight of her life. She endured years of physical and emotional abuse and, like many of us, told no one. One weekend her abuser went away and she knew she had to leave the house because she had a sense that he, or someone he would hire, would come to kill her (he had threatened to have her killed many times). She couldn't tell her family or friends, so she told a neighbor, half joking, but the neighbor took it seriously and encouraged her to go to a shelter.

She went to a women's shelter where the staff helped her get on her feet. She had been financially tied to her abuser and he used that as a prison—repeatedly telling her she would never survive without him. But she got out of the shelter and kept relatively quiet for fear that he would come looking for her. She and her children painstakingly made a full separation from him over the next year. In that time, her abusive ex married again and had a baby.

Then her worst nightmare came true: He murdered his new wife and baby then took his own life. She felt horrified but validated. This was the only way she would ever be truly set free. With him dead. Because as long as he was alive, she always feared what he could do to her, and she was never legally allowed to tell her story.

When I look back over the two years I was involved with John, I know why I stayed. I wanted to prove to him and to myself that I was worth loving. I wanted to be the one who changed him and saved him from himself. I had cheated on him in the first month or so of our relationship, and we never recovered from it. I thought his abuse was because of my choice, but he would have been abusive even had I not made that choice. The history of infidelity (if you can even call it that when two people are long-distance dating for a few weeks) just made it easier for him to abuse me.

During our two-year relationship, John was the master and I was the puppet. He tracked my every move by GPS tag, and if I didn't check in with photos and videos to substantiate my whereabouts, I was immediately charged with cheating. Now I know that John, like the woman in Texas's ex, had been abused in his childhood. Abuse begets abuse. This doesn't make it right, but it does explain a lot. John's abusive tendencies were heightened by his drug use.

I knew that John was a smoker when we first started dating. What I quickly began to realize was that he wasn't just smoking cigarettes. The daily use of marijuana didn't bother me that much and sometimes I liked a half-baked John; it seemed to mellow him out. Edibles and bong hits would have been fine, but pot was only his baseline.

A few months into our relationship I started paying closer attention. We lived in different cities, so our relationship was long distance, and almost always, John would travel for work, and I would drop everything and meet him in whatever city he happened to be in.

At the start of a trip together, I began seeing a pattern. He would wake up, pound caffeine, and pop a pill. In my naïveté, I thought it was a vitamin. Turns out it was an upper. Then he would smoke some pot to take it all down a notch. If that didn't work, he would take a beta-blocker. From there it was up and down with a myriad of orange bottles that seemed to be hidden everywhere. He had a doctor who would give him pretty much whatever he wanted. I don't know exactly what he was taking, but I'd see his mood shift dramatically from hour to hour. No matter where we were on the globe, I was always traveling with Jekyll, Hyde, and at least three other characters.

Every trip began the same way. We were great when we were great. But somewhere during the latter half of the first day, John's eyes would glaze over. His stare would turn from loving and caring to that of a cold and frightening monster. He would start persecuting me. And I would start crying. Then we would fight. And the remaining three days would be the roller coaster from hell. He would drop me off at the airport, my eyes swollen from days of crying. I would get to my gate, and like clockwork, my phone would ring and he would reverse course. Back to nice John. Back to "I love you." Back to "We will get through this." When I turned my phone on after landing back in Chicago, it would always be flooded with panicked, desperate texts from John apologizing for his terrible behavior. He would promise that it would never be like that again. But it always was. And every time it got worse.

There are so many stories . . . I could write an entire book on emotional abuse. But one story stands out. We were driving from Chicago to John's place. I can't tell you where he lived (for legal reasons) but it was far. My dog, Otis, had never really been a fan of the car, but since I planned to be gone for such a long time, I wanted to bring him with me on the road trip. I went to the vet and asked for medication so he could zone out and relax on our journey. John, Otis, and I took off and the trip was a great success—for about four hours. Then the attacks started. Usually this meant I was in for hours of interrogation and never-ending conversations that went in circles. But on this day something different happened. In the midst of an attack, John, who was driving, stopped his rapid-fire accusations. I looked over and saw that he was drooling. I asked if he felt okay, and with slurred speech he said we should pull over. When we were on the exit ramp, he rear-ended the car in front of us. I looked at him and his eyes had rolled back in his head.

"John?! John!"

For a split second I thought he was having a seizure. Or a heart attack. But my mind quickly registered the fact that my opioid-addicted boyfriend was likely suffering from an overdose.

"What did you take?"

His eyes rolled.

I shook him as the people got out of the car that we had rear-ended.

"John, WHAT DID YOU TAKE?"

He came to just enough to inform me: "The dog's pills."

He had taken one of Otis's tranquilizers. I quickly googled and the results were daunting. The dose for dogs, because their livers process drugs differently from humans, could be up to twelve times the strength of a human dose. And John had taken a whole pill.

Thankfully there was no serious damage, and I was able

to talk the nice couple we had rear-ended into not calling the police. After that was smoothed over, I told John we were going to have to get a hotel room and let him sleep off the drug. I was shaken and genuinely worried about John. I thought about calling a hospital, but through his slurred speech he demanded that I just get us to a hotel. The adrenaline was wearing off from our near-death highway experience and the fatigue led me to agree. Selfishly I figured I would get one full night of sleep without being verbally beaten up.

I was wrong. John woke up in the middle of the night when just enough of the canine tranquilizer had worn off and turned his anger all on me. It was my fault that we had to drive with the dog, my fault that the dog needed medication, and of course, my fault that John had to take a dose . . . because, you know, I'd cheated almost two years before. Thankfully he passed out again and I called Alysha to vent. Through my high-pitched blubbering, I finally paused long enough to hear her groggy voice. Concurrently I looked at the clock and realized it was 2:30 a.m. I had woken her up and she had just had a baby. She calmed me down, listened to the story, but then got very stern with me.

"Ging, this is approximately the thousand-and-first call in the middle of the night I have fielded from you because John has treated you so poorly. I hate hearing my friend like this, and honestly, I hate being your friend when you are like this.

You're not you anymore. You are his. Please get rid of him once and for all or we will not be able to be friends any longer. Call me when he is gone."

That hit me hard, but not hard enough. When John woke up in the morning, he was ready to drive again and we finished the trip to his place. Of course, I would never tell him about the phone call or the ultimatum. He never wanted to be around my family or friends anyway. He always kept me isolated so he could continue the abuse in private. A classic move by abusers.

We had a typical dramatic week at John's house (I wanted to call Alysha but knew I couldn't), and as I was packing to leave, I started frantically looking for Otis's pills. I couldn't find them anywhere. As soon as John got back from work, I asked him if he had seen them. He said, yes, and that he had taken them all.

He looked at me with a warning in his eyes that said, *Don't challenge me because this is all your fault.* All my fault that over the past four days he had taken all of my dog's travel medication. Right. And now Otis had none and would have to quiver and whine the whole trip back to Chicago. We drove back with poor Otis panting the whole way, and I, weak and abused as I was, just let it happen. I hate myself for that. That beautiful dog deserved only the best and that demon took that from him. I lost my best friend for a month, too, because

I couldn't get rid of John. I was still convinced that he was my future.

Thankfully I did get out of the relationship, but I will say I still have remnants of the abuse coursing through my relationships. I still question my value in my personal life and in my career, thanks to John. I grew up sensitive to criticism, but being with him took it to another level. At work I was becoming a master of bouncing viewers' awful comments off me, but in my personal life I was getting worse at being able to separate from him. I believed what he told me. He often told me I wasn't *really* a scientist despite my education. He challenged me and said that only PhDs are real scientists. That without doing research I could never claim that I was a scientist. He told me all the work I was doing was pointless, and that I was not even good at not being a scientist.

It would be a month before I finally pulled myself together and got away for good. In that time, I learned how crucial it was to have a team around me. That's what we have to talk about next.

CHAPTER SEVENTEEN
A LONG ROAD AHEAD

When I lived in Flushing during that first job at WEYI, we had a stalker at the TV station. He was especially keen on our main anchor on the weekends, Erin Looby. His obsession with her transferred at times to other reporters and anchors, and eventually included me. We would often see him just standing and staring at us at a local gas station, or at the Birch Run shopping center, where we often went to pick up dinner at KFC, Subway, or Taco Bell. There was not much the police could do, but we reported each of the encounters, and this was my indoctrination into the strange world of being a "public figure."

I've always hated that term. It sounds so generic. Like *resident* or *motorist*: words that just strip the personality from the humans they are meant to describe.

Those encounters were not just an introduction into the

world of TV but were also responsible for some serious nightmares that I later found out were part of my sleep paralysis, and mirrored the sleep paralysis I had suffered my sophomore year at Valparaiso.

In my nightmare, the stalker would not only capture me; he would put me in the trunk of his car. Each time the kidnapping went further and the tortures got darker. Eventually the nightmare progressed to the point where he had me back at my house. On my bed he would hold my shoulders down with a grip so tight I would wince at the virtual pain. He would forcefully sit on top of me, clasping my wrists with his strong hands to the bed, making them like handcuffs. I remember feeling almost awake, but I couldn't move.

In the final form of the nightmare, he put both my hands together above my head and reached down to the side of my bed to pull out a drill with a long bit. His mouth would get so close to my ear as he told me to hold still. Be quiet. That it wouldn't hurt as bad as I thought. He would put the drill bit to my forehead, my chest, and my belly button, teasing me by revving up the drill before quieting it and tapping it to a different part of my body.

I couldn't move even though I was awake. My arms and legs felt paralyzed and numb, and it would often take me minutes to shake the feeling that all of the dream was real.

I probably had this dream a dozen times. I didn't connect it to the narcolepsy I'd been diagnosed with the year before.

But at my next doctor's visit to get my medication, he asked if I had experienced any changes. I described the nightmare and the feeling of not being able to move. He told me that sleep paralysis was exactly what I was describing and that it was not at all uncommon for narcoleptics. He also told me that the content of my nightmare was particularly alarming, and I might want to see a therapist. I ignored that part, of course. I also lied on my medical form when it asked if I had ever been hospitalized or treated for mental illness.

To treat my narcolepsy, the doctor suggested I try another drug called GHB. You can't get GHB if you have a history of suicide attempts. But as far as that doctor knew, I didn't. Once I picked the drug up from the pharmacy, I followed the directions to a T. You had to prepare the doses and mix the first and second one at the same time. You took the first dose and placed the liquid of the second dose next to your bedside because your body would know when to wake you to take the second. Like a mummy without a memory, that is exactly what happened that night. The first dose went down easy. No flavor—it just tasted like water. I don't remember taking the second dose, but I woke up feeling groggy. Not hung-over but groggy. My state was reminiscent of the morning in that random dorm room in 2000. Like the morning I woke up in Flint with no memory of the previous night and I would turn out to be pregnant.

I have been working through this with Dr. Wilson and

he has explained that rape victims often don't remember any-thing from the rape, even if they aren't drugged. It is the mind's defense mechanism to block the memories so we can survive after an attack. But our minds were there, we were there, and those feelings of helplessness, being overpowered and con-trolled can show up in other ways. This realization did not in any way fix my problem, nor does it explain away choices I made in the years after these events, but it was enlightening.

As Dr. Wilson described this to me, we both realized that the trigger for my nightmares might have been the stalker, but the feelings, of being held down, of being "drilled" against my will . . . those might have all come from something that actu-ally happened in my past.

That's the kind of realization I am coming to in Dr Wilson's chair. It's one of the main reasons I still go to our sessions; during the pandemic, I have been even more con-sistent about seeing Dr. Wilson every Tuesday. While I was writing my first book, I wasn't seeing him. I had gotten to a manageable place with my depression and didn't think it was necessary.

After the book came out and I started writing this one, I realized how much more healing I needed, and now that I am wrapping up this book, I realize I have still only scratched the surface.

My colleague Dan Harris has talked in his books about meditation being the next big awakening in health. The treadmill for our mind. If meditation is the cardio, the strength training is going to be therapy—the breaking down of different parts of our brain and then making them stronger. In extreme conditions, just as it is for extreme weight loss and lifestyle changes, in-patient rehabilitation may be necessary.

There are dozens of kinds of therapy intended to treat different things. Dr. Wilson specializes in TFP or transference-focused psychotherapy. It's especially effective in treating borderline personality disorder. Which, surprisingly to me, is what his colleague diagnosed me with back in the hospital. Because—get this—I even thought that I met Dr. Wilson *at* the hospital. Granted, Columbia's mental hospital is not Club Med, so I was probably intentionally blocking something out, but apparently, that's where I was diagnosed and *referred* to Dr. Wilson. I was a master of blocking.

Either way, Dr. Wilson's TFP was pivotal in my healing. I don't think I had ever been properly diagnosed prior to that hospital visit, always labeled with depression, and never properly treated. So, as wonderful as Dr. Wilson is, he is also, actually, the first therapist performing a therapy meant to treat my particular disorder.

There's a series of true-or-false questions I had to answer in order for the doctors to assess my situation. There are several categories of the disorder and I was considered "moderate" at the time I was diagnosed. Here's a look:

My relationships are very intense, unstable, and alternate between the extremes of over-idealizing and undervaluing people who are important to me.

My emotions change very quickly, and I experience intense episodes of sadness, irritability, and anxiety or panic attacks.

My level of anger is often inappropriate, intense, and difficult to control.

Now, or in the past, when upset, I have engaged in recurrent suicidal behaviors, gestures, threats, or self-injurious behavior such as cutting, burning, or hitting myself.

I have a significant and persistently unstable image or sense of myself, or of who I am or what I truly believe in.

I have very suspicious ideas, and am even paranoid (falsely believe that others are plotting to cause me harm) at times; or I experience episodes under stress when I feel that I, other people, or the situation is somewhat unreal.

I engage in two or more self-damaging acts such as excessive spending, unsafe and inappropriate sexual conduct, substance abuse, reckless driving, and binge eating.

I engage in frantic efforts to avoid real or imagined abandonment by people who are close to me.

I suffer from chronic feelings of emptiness and boredom.

Identity is something that you give yourself. It has to do with what you stand for, morals, values, etc. It is who you are physically and legally, but that's just a basic *you already know that* statement.

Personality is the way in which you portray or "live in" your identity.

Borderline personality disorder sounds scary. People don't really know what it is and it isn't diagnosed all that often. Dr. Wilson says that is also a disorder that I have grown out of. I know that writing these books has helped me. Our identity is formed by other people's views of us and our views of ourselves. This book forced me to not only think about my truest narrative, which helps inform a healthy sense of identity, but also to work through it. I have learned so many tools for regulating my emotions, which then drive my actions as a wife, mother, and meteorologist.

For years, I thought it was my parents' fault, the chaos. Now I think so much can be understood by opening up to the real pain, shame, and guilt after I was raped and then again after my abortion. I only got to this better place by being honest about the trauma. Not using the easy escape and explanations of blaming my parents.

I mean, it makes perfect sense that less than a year after I had my abortion, I would find a stable, loving man and dive into a serious relationship with him. We got engaged within months. We were twenty-three. I never said this out loud, but I wanted everyone to know I was a good, stand-up woman. I wanted the husband and family that I was worried I was not going to have because I'd had an abortion.

I prayed to God and apologized all the time, always hoping that he wouldn't punish me by not letting me have children. When I found Joe, I felt like I could change my heart and my story. But as that wedding date approached, reality did, too. And if you read my first book, you know that I called it all off three weeks before we were set to walk down the aisle.

Then I was a "slut" who'd had an abortion and "broken a beautiful man's heart." My labels began defining me. I didn't know it then but that is a classic sign of borderline personality disorder. Your narrative about yourself changes rapidly. One day I was confident and didn't brand myself as anything negative; the next day I would let my horrible words drive even more horrible actions. That roller coaster propelled me into many unrealistic romantic relationships that I knew would never result in joy. I finally actually lived the promiscuous lifestyle I had labeled myself as living.

And ultimately, I became the perfect candidate for abuse. Instead of putting myself down, nearly killing myself, I would let someone else do it slowly.

So here I am, finally realizing all of this and beginning the process of forgiving myself for real. It was unfair for me to just assume God wouldn't forgive me, too. Because that's what he does—forgive.

A lot of people have written to me about faith. I was a student at a Lutheran university when I was raped. My faith was altered then. I was living alone in Flint, Michigan, when I had my abortion. I have not found God in the same way I was getting to know him back then, but in a far more spiritual way. I still believe in God. I still believe there is a higher power, a creator of the sun and earth. I am not certain what that is exactly, or if it's even a human form. But I am no longer going to operate as if I don't have any power.

I do have it. And I *can* forgive myself. It's going to take time, but now that I am aware, I think that gets me halfway there.

The only label I wish I would have gotten sooner was the diagnosis. I am Ginger Zee, I had borderline personality disorder, anorexia, and depression. Thanks to my therapy, I have finally found healing, and I would say I am recovered. But I know it takes hard work to stay in recovery. I am now at the most peaceful point I have felt on this planet, and I could not be more grateful.

Before the pandemic, I was nearing a point of overcommitment I often get to. A point at which I actually wished to suffer a minor injury that would give me an excused absence from work and a break. And then the world stopped. During this pandemic, I have spent more time with Ben and the kids than I ever would have otherwise. I have really felt like our house is a home. I have found incredible joy in cooking. I am so grateful that I have been able to still work and collect a salary, unlike so many others, but even with all that, I still feel the crush of the unknown. The uncertainty that surrounds the coronavirus about when the world will get back to whatever normal will be. That uncertainty has cornered me and caused me to experience gray mornings of depression, but I have been able to whip out my tools and my team to fight it. I talk it out, I journal. I put in the work. It is far from sunshine and rainbows, but I am trying not only to know that the storms are necessary, but that I should put my hands up, open my mouth, and let the rain fall in. Embrace the suck of life.

CHAPTER EIGHTEEN
THE CLOUDS DON'T LAST FOREVER

My glasses were fogged and my face wet with tears as I ran up the stairs from my basement-studio setup after doing *Good Morning America*. I stared out the window watching my four-year-old son run through our yard flying a kite. I cried harder. How am I the lucky one?

Vowing to live in the moment, I went to change from the TV dress I had worn into my play clothes for the start of the weekend.

As soon as I walked into my closet another wave of emotion hit me and I crumpled onto the soft Berber carpeting. It was 9 a.m. and I just sat, slumped over, wailing, surrounded by shoes that hadn't been worn in months (thanks to the pandemic, I was still doing weather barefoot in my basement), my TV makeup streaming down my face with each release of tears.

My sorrow grew to joy, then back to grief and guilt, swinging wildly on both sides of the emotional pendulum that I pride myself on finally having found.

The impetus for this breakdown was all about one date: November 8, 2003.

It was suicide prevention week, so I had posted about my own suicide attempts and wanted to pass it forward to a friend and fellow advocate, Vonnie Woodrick. I had met Vonnie in 2018 when I spoke at her annual gala for i understand, a group that promotes the love of healing after someone dies by suicide. From that first meeting to the coffee and drink dates we have had since, I have found real friendship and inspiration in Vonnie and her story. She, like me, was ready to change the world of mental health.

Vonnie's book, *i understand*, covers not only her husband's death by suicide but most importantly, the love that still helps heal her. It's a quick read. I was skimming back through the book to find a quote to post—that's when I came across that date. November 8, 2003.

Vonnie's husband had hanged himself. She found him. The paramedics tried to save him and they spent four days in the hospital before they took him off the ventilator.

Four days. That means Vonnie came into the hospital on November 4, 2003. I left the hospital on November 4, 2003, after my suicide attempt.

I walked out alive. Rob didn't.

Why? How? It was the same hospital. We both lived in Grand Rapids.

Vonnie, a woman I have worked with and befriended, a woman who has petitioned to redefine suicide—not as the dictionary describes it (the intentional taking of one's own life), but rather as a terminal side effect of mental illness—that same woman was at the same hospital the same day I was released after my suicide attempt.

I wrote Vonnie an urgent email, realizing that I somehow didn't have her cell-phone number. She called immediately and listened to me explaining myself through choking tears.

We both know the reason we had this sliding-door moment—this moment at all—was so we could help others not have to end up taking their own lives.

I told Vonnie that it wasn't just the coincidence at the hospital that had stunned me and left me leaving in my closet—it was the thought of how many other families were in the hospital that day, that week . . . how common suicide is.

We have to make this better.

A few days later I was off to cover Hurricane Sally and Vonnie sent this:

> Hi Ginger,
>
> I've thought so much these past couple days about our conversation and our experience on Nov. 4th 2003.

*You walked out, a changed person. You went on
to live such a beautiful life with so many wonderful
unknowns and challenges along the way. You also
became and have the power to be the "tornado through
stigma"—reducing judgement and stigma, finding the
power in sharing stories, and are committed to making a
difference. Thank you for that.*

*You are changing lives while I'm sure, healing
your own.*

*I walked in on November 4th with my husband and
walked out, four days later without him. The journey
has been long and difficult yet I know Rob has been
by my side every step of the way. Perhaps, even having
something to do with connecting us.*

*Rob gave me the gift of passion, a trait that I so
admired in him. We share that passion. You . . . have
touched my heart in so many ways. Love heals and
comes from the most unexpected places. You . . . are an
unexpected place. Thank you for sharing you with me,
more clarity came after our emotional conversation the
other day. The journey continues to become clear.*

♥ *Vonnie*

That clarity, it's coming to me, too. All these obstacles,
even with my privilege—they are all a part of *this* story—the

story that will hopefully help keep someone else out of the hospital. Or get them there before it's too late. Or maybe even create a place where people can go, a mental-health rehab available to all. My narrative needs to be shared so others can know it is okay to live theirs openly and freely.

Vonnie's letter made me think back to my breakthrough moment. Ten months after my hospital stay and commitment to healing, I had the "the moment." I describe this as the opposite of when people say they are having "a moment," as that usually implies unwarranted drama—but this was "the moment" in that I was finally feeling and allowing myself to feel. The moment I remember my identity diffusion beginning to fuse again.

I had packed my bags for Nepal prior to taking a work trip. I needed new passport photos for my visa, so my now husband and then boyfriend had accompanied me to a CVS on the Upper West Side. We walked through the aisles hoping the line would diminish at the photo counter. I grabbed the deodorant I needed and a travel-size bottle of shampoo. Ben and I held hands and I felt him looking at me once we planted ourselves in line.

There, next to an Entenmann's donut display, in the line for photos, he blurted out: "I love you."

Unlike other relationships in the past, I had not gone to "I love you" too soon and I did not recoil when he said it.

Instead, my eyes stayed soft and my lips curled into a smile. I felt real, measured love. And I replied, "I love you, too."

It was the most natural exchange of I-love-you's I had ever experienced. It was grounded and authentic and far from lust-filled.

I should have known my "moment" was coming from that preview. But I had no idea how crystal clear and sunny life was about to get.

Opening the window shade on the Qatar Airways flight before we slowly descended into Kathmandu, I could see the ground was dry but the grasses and trees were lush and green. In a very short time, this sparsely populated land had become nearly treeless. Millions of rooftops, colored tarps, dirt and paved roads intersected and wound around a city that from above looked dense and dizzying. I blinked my eyes dramatically, blaming the lack of clarity I was seeing on the whirlwind thirty hours of travel from New York to Doha to Kathmandu. I had been with ABC for less than a year and a half, so my pitch was a big one. I told them I would do anything, even take the coach middle seat on several flights, to get there for two days, turn around, and come back. Anything so I could tell the story of the rapid decline of the vulture population. Yes, vultures. As horrid as these animals' reputation may be, they have a real place on our planet and in the circle of life, especially in this part of Nepal, where monks lay out the bodies of the dead instead of cremating or burying them. Vultures are vital, and something—which turned out to be a toxin injected in cows—was killing them by the thousands.

Perhaps you haven't been in a news-reporting setting, but the pitch as I just wrote it would have never gotten me on a flight to the other side of the world. So instead, I pitched it this way:

"Hey, guys! How cool would it be if I jumped off the Himalayas and a bird ate from my hand? I want to tell a story about para-hawking—a new eco-tourism trend that is bringing attention to endangered species."

That sounded much more GMA.

And it worked.

As I was nodding my head and thinking about how unbelievably lucky I was to have a job that allowed me to make such a pitch, a line of thunderstorms in the distance caught my eye. Gazing out the window again, I was enchanted by the tops of the cumulonimbus clouds, and my brain started working overtime to try to figure out what geographically or atmospherically could be inducing high tops like I was seeing . . . and then I realized . . . *Oh my goodness, those are mountains. Not just any mountains—the Himalayas.* The Himalaya mountains make *majestic* sound like a dim word.

While I was marveling at their majesty the plane landed. The tires hit the tarmac, people gathered their things, and I felt like I was entering a movie set. As soon as I walked off the jetway I was met by a small child. Big brown eyes, beautiful raven hair so shiny I wanted to reach out and see if it felt as silky as it looked. I glanced around to see if my producer Niels was there to meet me (I had traveled alone) before my eyes settled back on the little girl and her tattered shoes, dusty shorts, and flower top. She stared up at me with a devilish grin and abruptly threw red powder paint in my face.

"Pppff." I blew out as one does when shockingly pied in the face or, I guess the equivalent of a pie in the face in Nepal, pelted with powdered paint. By the time I had rubbed my eyes free, the cutest little paint perpetrator was gone. Vanished.

Niels approached, laughing. He informed me that it was Holi—the festival of spring for Hindus. Our friend and fellow producer Nick rounded the corner to join us. Both Nick and Niels had also been adorned with different-colored paint. I smiled, hugged them, and we rounded up my things. As I looked around the baggage claim, I could smell the earth of this place. The age. It felt like living history, but at the same time, especially with the festivities happening around us, it felt so alive. When I look back at the photo of Nick and me covered in that paint, it brings good tears to my eyes. My smile is real. Like genuine happiness was starting to come out. Joy. Something I don't think I had felt through and through for a decade.

As we traveled to our hostel in the farm town where we would be shooting the story, I noticed the slow pace, the calm and fresh sanctity in the air. This was a part of the world I never knew I would have a chance to see. Like most work trips, my time was limited; even though I had flown around the world to be here, I only had two days to shoot the story, so we got started right away.

We drove to a sanctuary where Scott Mason was utilizing a few trained vultures to bring awareness to the plight of these creatures. Scott introduced me to Bob and Kevin, two Egyptian vultures that looked more like fancy seagulls with a comical puff of white feathers surrounding their heads. They were among the species of vultures that had lost 99.9 percent of their population. After learning a few basics of falconry, we piled into a small taxi, Niels and I in the back, Kevin and Scott in the passenger seat. Kevin, the bird, did not look at us; he just stayed focused on the road. As if being in this otherworldly country wasn't enough, now I was riding in a taxi with a vulture.

We exited the car and everyone put on their backpacks and gear to hike the paragliders up the rest of the mountain. At about five thousand feet there was a vast opening. I had done this drill a few times before in Colombia and Mexico while covering paragliding. I just had never done it with the intent of flying with a vulture. This was not just paragliding; this was para-hawking.

Pokhara is known for its magical air: so easy to paraglide in—so perfect for what seems like an inhuman ability. It makes sense this is where I would actually find my mental wings. I was more than a year into my dream job, but I was also just over a year into my true healing. The tools I had learned during my hospital stay and after that stay with Dr. Wilson were starting to take root. I had been watering and feeding those roots, and this April adventure was the perfect fertilizer to make my feelings bloom. The petals of feelings I may have had since I was a child had always been stomped on, starved, or plucked before they had a chance to absorb the rays of and bask in the sun. Here, I could tell the bloom was happening, and I was going to give it free rein.

After a few tests using a falconry glove and actual meat, the wind started to shift. We got ourselves situated in the paraglider, then waited—there is a lot of waiting at the beginning of paragliding because you have to have consistency in the wind speed so you don't plummet off the mountainside when you take off. I looked down at the straps of the paraglider and stared at my light-coral Lululemon long-sleeved top. It had been a gift from Ben before I left. I had cried when he gave it to me. Another sign that those feeling flowers were blooming.

His reaction when I started crying was to use humor because most people would not cry over a new shirt. I was crying because I had never had a partner in my life who cared enough to send me off on a work adventure with a new, perfect-for-TV top. This partner was the first that I had been fully honest with—Ben heard it all—and he still loved me. He was like a dictionary in my quest to write my own narrative that would include love and a healthier balance of emotions. I had never had a man invest time into making sure I felt respected and who communicated so openly. That shirt wasn't what made me cry. (I mean, it was nice, and I love Lulu.) *I* made me cry, or should I say, I allowed myself to cry. As I reflected on this beautiful yet odd moment with Ben, as I looked at the bright color of my shirt, I was jarred by Niels's call. "Let's go."

Scott and I scrambled to our feet—he was behind me and would be manning the flight controls so I could experience the flight with Kevin, who would find us in the air, I was told.

Scott asked if I was ready to run, and I looked right into the GoPro camera on the end of the stick in my free hand.

"Never been more ready," I announced.

Scott nonchalantly said, "One, two, three, we go."

And off the edge of the Himalayas we ran. There was a second or two of falling, then *whoosh*—the wind grabbed our wing and we were flying. The first turns up aren't necessarily smooth, but within thirty seconds the peacefulness of paragliding washed over me. If you've never been, it's a must. There is no roller-coaster-like fear, but rather peaceful gliding.

I inhaled deeply, taking in the air thousands of feet up in that atmosphere that I love so much. When I knew the severe turns were leveling out and I wouldn't risk getting airsick, I looked down.

There was a large lake glistening below us and it got smaller as we flew higher, but I could still make out the cows and the boys leading them with their sticks. I could still see how glasslike the lake below was with the reflection of the mountains. It was a Bob Ross painting, complete with happy little trees. *Happy.* There was that word again. That feeling. Another petal bloomed.

And at that instant, Scott, who was behind me operating the tandem paraglider, told me to stretch out my arm and prepare with a piece of meat in my gloved hand. Kevin came swooping in from behind us. I could feel him before he even landed. The grip of his talons was tight but brief, his reach for the raw meat almost dainty. He sat for only a moment, looked at me, and then flew off. And we followed. Flying the same thermals and pockets of heat that he was.

I had never understood the science of the atmosphere better than when I started paragliding.

As the vulture took off, a sensation shot through me. It trumped the camera on my toe and the camera looking at me—in the most public of settings, I felt a tear of joy roll down my face, cutting through the thick makeup I had applied to hide my jet-lagged eyes and skin. That tear felt so full, so large and meaningful, because it held all my petals.

I was feeling. And I was okay with feeling. And although it took this extreme experience for me to truly break through, I knew right there that the man that I had said "I love you" to just forty-eight hours before would be my husband. I knew that we would have a family together. I finally believed there was sunshine in this world and that I was allowed to bask in it. And I knew that I deserved happiness. I finally knew that what I said and did had purpose and deserved to be said and done. And I was allowed to feel it all. I also knew that I was grateful for the sadness and loneliness and intense pain that had filled my life. I knew this was the moment in which I embraced feelings. And let them fly. Like Kevin the vulture and I had flown.

As my epiphany unfolded on that flight, the landing taught me something even more important. There are many ways you can land in paragliding. Some are very gentle and almost lift you back up. Others are like the type I had experienced in Colombia in a burnt-out sugarcane field where divots in the farmland below became part of our unplanned landing strip, and we had to lift our legs in order to avoid breaking them at such a fast speed. We tumbled and rolled on that occasion.

But this landing in Pokhara that day was as serene as the moment in the air had been. Scott announced that we would be taking it down quickly so we could get in another run for video purposes. I watched as the boys with the sticks, the cows, the people in the town, and the lake all got bigger and in better focus. I saw a group of children gathering at the landing strip where we had targeted.

As we approached, Scott gave me a countdown and I didn't even need to take steps. We kissed the ground gently and with ease, the wing of the paraglider softly collapsing behind us as the children who had watched these "aliens" dropping from above ran to us and hugged us. Smiles so big and bright. The feelings were unbelievable. This was joy. I was feeling. I was alive. And unlike the jumps I had done in the past, this was not just a jump to search for my purpose or because "who cares what happens"—this was a jump into my life. This was a safe and free landing in so many more ways than the literal. And I couldn't wait to do it all again.

That's the feeling I wake up with most days.

I want to do it again. I want to keep jumping into my life; even when there is a disaster, I want to be there. No helicopter. All petals. All feeling. I want to bask in that sunlight when it's there because I know better than anyone: The storms don't last forever; they can't and they won't. It's not how the atmosphere works and it's not how life works.

Acknowledgments

A t one point, Samantha Wnek had more photos of me on her phone than she did of her own family. She knows my schedule and remembers my life in more detail than I ever could ("Hey Sam—I got married on June 7, right?" "Yes Ginger." is an annual conversation). I've followed the heels of her iridescent shell shoes around the world. She's the silent partner who never requires attention but desperately deserves at least half of the accolades I get in my life. Bottom line, I don't know if I could function without my sister, friend, and producer, meteorologist Samantha Wnek.

Meteorologist Max Golembo is the second man I wake up to—the guy who is in my ear keeping it all together on GMA. My "no-man" who most days I appreciate—and on other days, I appreciate after we are done debating.

To the woman who has kept my hair looking right—with the best attitude—my nineties hip-hop dancing superstar turned hair stylist and hype woman, Merylin Mitchell.

The team in the thick of it now making me look good from GMA to World News Tonight to It's Not Too Late: Chris Donato, Daniel Manzo, Daniel Peck, Melissa Griffin, Tony Morrison, Scott Kolbicz, Lindsey Griswold, Stephanie Ebbs,

Jon Schlosberg, Andrew Lear, Cleo Andreadis, Rick Sures, Jay Sures, and Jenna Fogelman. For Caragh Fisher and Kerry Smith, for always looking out for me even if I like to push it.

My best friends, Alysha, Kelley, Liz, and Lindsey. Brad Edwards, for always being the sounding board, the guy I call when I don't want to smoke a cigarette and the one pushing me to be a better writer but more importantly a better mother and wife.

And Wendy Lefkon—thanks for believing in me and for being that unicorn of a woman who truly supports another woman.

To Abby Smith, our nanny and basically the third parent in our family, unending gratitude.

To my parents, whom I can't be more grateful for—I'm sorry for the blame I put on you for so long. Thank you for loving me through it all. You have done such a great job as parents.

To those little boys that steal my heart each and every day. The pride I have, the bursting joy you bring, and the lessons you teach me every day, my little peaches—Adrian and Miles—you're my boys.

And to my husband—for always capturing me at my worst, sharing that, and making me know that's still the best. Making me see and feel the love for myself that you feel for me. My heart—my bean—I love you.